Pulling Strings

Linda Pembroke Kaiser

Clark Irish Harp

To Dave —
For all you do
for music in our
community.
Happy Holidays —
Lynne
12/2011

Pulling Strings

The Legacy of
Melville A. Clark

LINDA PEMBROKE KAISER

With a Foreword by Dennis Connors

SYRACUSE UNIVERSITY PRESS

For a listing of books published and distributed by Syracuse University Press,
visit our Web site at SyracuseUniversityPress.syr.edu.

ISBN: 978-0-8156-0950-6

Library of Congress Cataloging-in-Publication Data
Kaiser, Linda P.
    Pulling strings : the legacy of Melville A. Clark / Linda Pembroke Kaiser ;
with a foreword by Dennis Connors. — 1st ed.
        p. cm.
    Includes bibliographical references and index.
    ISBN 978-0-8156-0950-6 (cloth : alk. paper)
  1. Clark, Melville. 2. Harp makers—United States—Biography.
3. Harpists—United States—Biography. 4. Celtic harp—United States—
History. 5. Inventors—United States—Biography. I. Title.
    ML424.C55K37 2010
    780.92—dc22
    [B]   2010005643

Manufactured in the United States of America

Whatsoever thy hand findeth to do,
do it with all thy might;
for there is no work, nor device,
nor knowledge, nor wisdom,
in the grave, whither thou goest.
—Ecclesiastes 9:10

LINDA PEMBROKE KAISER is a musician who performs on the harp, piano, and guitar. She has published articles in the *International Folk Harp Journal* and an album of harp music, *Lullabies for Earth Children,* for two harps. She lives in Syracuse, New York, and near Mount Dora, Florida.

Contents

List of Illustrations   *ix*

Foreword, DENNIS CONNORS   *xiii*

Preface   *xvii*

Acknowledgments   *xix*

Clark Family Tree   *xxi*

1. Melville Clark: *The Man and His Family*   *1*

2. The House That Clark Built   *14*

3. The Clark Irish Harp   *29*

4. Birth of the Nylon Harp String   *54*

5. Inventions and Ideas   *62*

6. The First Syracuse Symphony Orchestra   *75*

7. Singing Troops and War Balloons   *96*

8. White House Connections   *105*

9. The Collections   *113*

Final Note   *137*

APPENDIX A. Publications by Melville A. Clark   *141*

APPENDIX B. Serial Numbers and Manufacture Dates
for Clark Irish Harps   *143*

APPENDIX C. Cost of Manufacture of the Clark Irish Harp   *145*

Notes   *163*

Selected Bibliography   *179*

Index   *181*

Illustrations

Color Plates

Following page 74
Uncle Melville Clark
Melville Clark on the cover of *Piano Trade Magazine*
Elaine Vito, NBC harpist, playing the harp underwater
Sales tag for the Clark Fruit Picker
Publicity for Prokofieff's concert
Cover of souvenir program from the Song and Light Festival
Stamps from many countries
Cover of Schirmer-Clark catalog

Figures

Father and mother of Melville A. Clark   *2*
Clark family   *3*
Clark children at harps   *4*
Melville Clark with an Erard harp   *6*
Harp ensemble at the Twelfth Annual National Harp Festival   *7*
Travelers' and Drovers' Tavern   *9*
Clark family trailer trip to Cape Cod, Massachusetts   *10*
Clarks at home at Travelers' and Drovers' Tavern   *11*
Melville Clark with Prescott cello   *12*
Clark Music storefront, shared with Krause Jewelry   *16*
George W. Clark with an Erard harp   *18*
Clark's piano- and harp-moving wagon   *19*
Clark's six-story music store   *20*
Apollo Recital Hall program   *22*

Clark Music Company broadcast over WSYR 23

Newsletter, *Hall O'Harps Monthly* 25

Melville Clark playing an early model of his harp 33

Clark Irish Harp patent drawing 35

Jobber's Agreement to sell the Clark Irish Harp 38

Professor Van Veachton Rogers 40

Clark's sketch of Timothy Clark Plastic (Fiberglass) Harp 45

Melville Clark on Mount Wilson, California 46

Postcard from C. E. Rofgren from Antarctica 47

Letter from Dr. F. Dana Coman from Antarctica 48

Ship photos of Dr. Coman 49

Citation from Rear Adm. Richard E. Byrd 50

Clark playing a concert harp strung with nylon strings 55

String-gauge list from R. H. Carter, du Pont 57

Melville Clark with four harps strung with nylon strings 58

Clark demonstrates the imperviousness of nylon strings to water 60

Clark Nylon Harp String packet 61

Letterhead of Melville Clark's "Ideas" stationery 63

Patent for Clark Fruit Picker invention 64

Patent drawing of the Clark Fruit Picker 65

Clark Music Co. letterhead used to promote sales of the
    Clark Fruit Picker 66

Telegram to Clark from Leopold Stokowski 70

Melville Clark with tone amplifier 71

First Syracuse Symphony Orchestra board officers 77

D. T. Brennan, Music Committee member 78

Syracuse Symphony Orchestra stationery, 1923–24 79

The Syracuse Symphony Orchestra with Dr. William Berwald,
    conductor 81

B. F. Keith Theatre interior 82

Tina Lerner, pianist 83

Vladimir Shavitch, conductor 84

Symphony's Watertown, New York, concert 89

Victor Miller, director 91

Professor André Polah, conductor 92

Conductor Nicholas Gualillo   *93*

Postcard of Syracuse Recruitment Camp   *97*

Margaret Wilson and Melville Clark at Camp May, New Jersey   *98*

British soldiers with propaganda balloons   *104*

Luncheon party at the 500 Club   *107*

Wilson party at the door of the auditorium   *109*

Margaret Wilson at Cornish, New Hampshire   *110*

White House Musicale program   *112*

Walter Welch and Melville Clark   *115*

List of discs for the music box   *117*

Letter from Buckingham Palace   *118*

Clark with Regina music box, cabinet, and discs   *119*

Clark amuses the plane crew en route to London   *121*

Clark arriving at Buckingham Palace   *121*

Lap piano   *126*

Clark playing a lap organ   *127*

Clark presenting a French harp to Henry Ford   *130*

Clark with the Cleopatra harp   *131*

Tiny Manchurian dove harp   *133*

Clark holding the musical bow with gourd resonator   *134*

Ethiopian harp made from wood and twigs   *135*

Tortoise shell strung with metal harp strings   *136*

Tables

1. Clark Irish Harp and taborette patents   *53*

2. Children's assembly plan   *171*

Foreword

DENNIS CONNORS

TODAY WE ARE INUNDATED with images from television. The medium enters our homes twenty-four hours a day, seven days a week. And the channel options presented by cable are staggering. There are probably people who have so many cable TV stations available on their sets that they haven't even found them all yet and perhaps never will.

With that current reality and the passing of years, the number of people who can remember a time when there was no television is shrinking daily. So it is hard for many to conjure up the anticipation, excitement, and wonder that the arrival of television broadcasting brought to America in the late 1940s.

In the case of the upstate New York municipality of Syracuse, with a population of nearly 220,000 at the time, that day came on December 1, 1948. And the first images that those Central New Yorkers saw, as few as they might have been given the limited number of televisions, was, of all things, a man playing a harp. For those who knew Melville Clark, it probably was no surprise at all.

Clark was local, and that WHEN broadcast originated in its pioneer studio on the city's North Side. But Clark was also a consummate promoter, both of his trade in the business of musical instruments and in his love for one in particular—the harp. That he would be playing his harp in that first fuzzy but historic television broadcast in Syracuse is just another captivating chapter in the saga of this fascinating figure.

Portions of Clark's busy, wide-ranging, and colorful life have been reported in past articles and brief mentions in musical histories. Until

xiii

now, though, there has not been a thorough exploration of his career. This book by Linda Kaiser corrects that omission with a wonderful, well-researched narrative that explores his numerous contributions to American musical history. She has mined a rich cache of Clark family papers, one group in private hands and another within the Special Collections division of Syracuse University's Library. And these holdings include a wealth of photographs and graphic materials of high quality that add significant visual interest to the story.

Clark was born in Syracuse in 1883 and spent his life in Central New York. His family business grew to be one of the nation's largest music stores, retailing a wide variety of instruments from its downtown location. The building was a well-known local landmark until its demolition in 1967. His business activities, civic involvement, and concert promotions in Syracuse were numerous and could fill a good-sized book on their own. But he also was a nationally recognized harpist, with a concert résumé that grew to thousands of performances, including several presidential recitals at the White House.

And yet one might argue that his most notable claim to fame was as the inventor and creative marketer of a distinctive small, easily portable and playable harp called the Clark Irish harp, manufactured in his hometown. This beautiful instrument, no longer well known by the average Syracusan, deserves to reside in the same historic "hall of fame" of Syracuse-made products as the Dietz lantern, the Franklin automobile, the Marsellus casket, the Syracuse Chilled Plow, and the Stearns bicycle.

Syracuse, still known today as the Salt City, has long carried that nickname, bestowed in memory of its founding industry. As salt manufacturing waned in the late nineteenth century, some citizens strongly suggested that a new industry—typewriter manufacturing— should supersede the white mineral and that the town be reclassified as "Typewriter City." After reading this story, however, one could make a good case that Melville Clark almost singlehandedly built a reputation centered in Syracuse that warranted this town be honored as the "Harp City."

Clearly, Clark's devotion to the harp, as musician, inventor, manufacturer, and marketer, makes his story appealing to anyone with affection for that evocative but somewhat mysterious instrument. Clark's persistent activity in bringing harp playing to an audience beyond the classical concertgoer is one to be admired. Playing the instrument in an early TV broadcast was one way, but he didn't begin or end there.

His creative imagination had him plucking strings in 1918 on the top of Mount Wilson in Southern California, on an airplane flight across the Atlantic in 1948, and in a submerged submarine the following year. In promoting his invention of nylon strings for the instrument, which were resistant to the vagaries of changing humidity, a long-standing annoyance to players, he arranged to have a female harpist play a few notes while completely immersed in a tank of water. That particular gig earned a color photograph in the December 13, 1948, edition of *Life* magazine. In his day, no one seems to have approached Clark in making the harp accessible to the average American, except perhaps, the man who once bore its name—Harpo Marx.

So we have in this work a series of wonderful tales of a talented, energetic man and his ever more intriguing ventures in promoting harp music to the masses. But there is embodied here an equally important documentation of the life of a local businessman and engaged citizen in an average American city during the first half of the twentieth century. This volume becomes, therefore, an important contribution to the study of the particular history of Syracuse, New York.

Modest-size American cities like Syracuse contain a wealth of historical materials that document their residents and the development and evolution of their communities. Local historical agencies and libraries are filled with the stuff, which is too often overlooked by academic historians. While certainly narratives that draw on these sources today may be of immediate interest to the locals, these stories are also rich examples of the American experience that can and should appeal to wider audiences. And Clark's life beyond harps was certainly one worth bringing to light. These include his "main street" commercial activities, his efforts to create a civic symphony for Syracuse, his business enterprises outside the musical world, and, interestingly, his own great appreciation for the preservation of history. Clark amassed a world-class collection of historic musical instruments and chose to renovate an early-nineteenth-century tavern outside of Syracuse as his home.

In older northeastern cities like Syracuse, ones that have faced economic challenges for a half century, there is an effort underway to attract what has been nicknamed the "creative class." This group is seen as one that will have the vision to uncover the new technologies and harness the needed entrepreneurship that will drive the engines of future economic health. It is a class that is drawn to and thrives in an urban environment with a good balance of culture, aesthetics, energetic lifestyles, and intellectual stimulation.

A century ago, Melville Clark was such a man, who both thrived in Syracuse and contributed greatly to its quality of life. For Central New Yorkers, harp enthusiasts, musical historians, or students of the American experience, Ms. Kaiser has offered a stimulating journey through the extraordinary life of one of our own.

Preface

ON A SUMMER'S EVENING in 1891, a young lad, his father, and a harp arrived at the stage door of the Old Bastable Theatre in upstate New York. It was amateur night. The youngster was seven and could barely reach the strings, but by standing on his tiptoes he was able to pluck the high notes. His solo debut was a huge success. He won first prize and three dollars. The son and his father were surprised and happy.

The boy was Melville A. Clark, and from that evening on he continued to make beautiful music for presidents and royalty, children and discerning audiences, in small parlors, large concert halls, churches, and military camps. Clark also became a pioneer in the musical and cultural life of Syracuse and beyond.

Among his most notable achievements, he was president and manager of the Clark Music Company, once the largest musical establishment in central New York. He was founder, in 1921, of the first Syracuse Symphony Orchestra and—perhaps his greatest claim to fame—designer of a portable Celtic-style harp.

Clark always made his home in upstate New York. He was born fewer than twenty years after the Civil War and lived through World Wars I and II. Though his formal education was fragmented, his family provided him with educational experiences in England, France, and Ireland to enhance his harp playing and harp building.

This study began as a lecture describing an early Irish harp builder in Syracuse, where I reside. However, as I learned more about Melville Clark, I began to write short stand-alone pieces about the various facets of his professional life. Combined here as a book, they portray a sparkling personage in three dimensions.

This book, then, is about Clark as musician, inventor, entrepreneur, educator, community leader, and collector. Though I have provided the basic details of Clark's life along with many personality-revealing stories, this account is concerned primarily with Clark's legacy, not with his development as a person; it is not a biography.

The research for this book is based on the papers of Melville A. Clark and the Clark Music Company, most of which were given in 1965 to Syracuse University Library's Special Collections Research Center. In 1993 Melville Clark Jr. turned over to me the remaining papers, photographs, and ephemera. Unless otherwise noted, the illustrations come from my own collection.

Among Clark's papers were twenty or more autobiographical pieces written for specific audiences of readers or listeners. Based on these writings, I am not sure whether Melville Clark would have liked to be remembered first as a businessman, or an inventor, or an educator, or even an important civic leader. The reader can decide whether Melville A. Clark was one of these terms—or, as he referred to himself, a "musician extraordinaire."

Acknowledgments

I HAVE MANY GOOD PEOPLE to thank for getting this book to completion.

In the beginning I gave an occasional lecture about the Clark harp, and made a few local TV appearances that led to three magazine articles, written to interest the folk harp world. It was a stroke of luck to be under the wing of a seasoned editor, and my thanks and praise go to Janie Taylor. Coincidentally, she too played the harp and as a child learned on a Clark. She said the writing was good and the stories interesting, and urged me for more.

I owe a debt of gratitude to fellow harpists for introducing me to the idea that Melville Clark was a person who really mattered: Elizabeth Kay, Patricia DeBottis, and Arsalaan Fay.

Staff members at Syracuse University Library's Special Collections Research Center who were especially helpful during the eighteen years I pored over the 175 boxes of archival papers: Diane Cooter, William La Moy, Bill Lee, and Kathleen Manwaring.

Also thanks goes to research assistant Rebekah Ambrose; Michael Flanagan, archivist at the Onondaga County Historical Association; and Daniel R. Smith, librarian at the Onondaga County Public Library.

Many knowledgeable persons helped me to validate facts and dates: Timothy and Melville Clark Jr., Nevart Apikian, Dale Barco, Murray Bernthal, Barbara Lane Buckland, Dick Case, Lucille Garlock, Donald House, Paul Knoke, Eileen McIntyre, Susan and Lance McKee, Samuel Milligan, Robert Sharp, Kenneth Williams, and Frank De Fonda of the Clark Music Company.

Thanks to those individuals who helped me in their own special way: Lynn Baker, Howard Bryan, Elizabeth Clark, Michele Combs, Betsy Fairbank, Elizabeth Hueber, Elizabeth Huntley, Nancy Hurrell, Gail Lyons, Ernest Muzquiz, Ruth Papalia, Myrna Partenza, Neva Pilgrim, Carole Taylor, and the Dorset Team.

Credit for the final manuscript making its way into print goes to Mary Beth Hinton, who stayed with the project to its completion.

Finally, I could not have completed this work without the help of my husband, Harvey, who took time from his own interests to become reader, critic, computer consultant, and an enabler on many levels.

Clark Family Tree

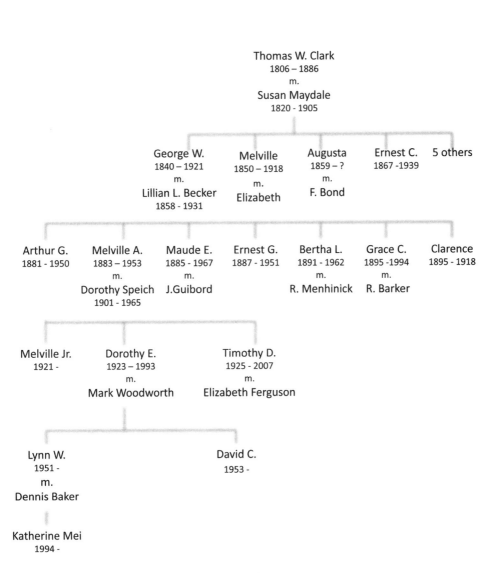

Thomas W. Clark
1806 – 1886
m.
Susan Maydale
1820 - 1905

George W.
1840 – 1921
m.
Lillian L. Becker
1858 - 1931

Melville
1850 – 1918
m.
Elizabeth

Augusta
1859 – ?
m.
F. Bond

Ernest C.
1867 -1939

5 others

Arthur G.
1881 - 1950

Melville A.
1883 – 1953
m.
Dorothy Speich
1901 - 1965

Maude E.
1885 - 1967
m.
J.Guibord

Ernest G.
1887 - 1951

Bertha L.
1891 - 1962
m.
R. Menhinick

Grace C.
1895 -1994
m.
R. Barker

Clarence
1895 - 1918

Melville Jr.
1921 -

Dorothy E.
1923 – 1993
m.
Mark Woodworth

Timothy D.
1925 - 2007
m.
Elizabeth Ferguson

Lynn W.
1951 -
m.
Dennis Baker

David C.
1953 -

Katherine Mei
1994 -

Pulling Strings

1

Melville Clark

The Man and His Family

IF IT TAKES A VILLAGE to raise a child, one might say it took three generations of four musical families to raise a musician extraordinaire. That person was Melville Clark. He was the second child born to George Waldo Clark and Lillian Becker Clark on September 12, 1883, in Syracuse, New York. He was named after his uncle Melville Clark, inventor of the Apollo player piano. Melville often signed his name with the middle initial "A." or used "Antone" to distinguish himself from his uncle.[1]

In 1880 George W. Clark married Lillian Becker, thereby uniting two of the most notable musical families in upstate New York during the period between the Civil War and the Victorian age. Lillian's father, Conrad Becker, was a Syracuse University orchestra conductor, a professor of music, and a concert zitherist. Her brother, Professor Conrad L. Becker, a professional violinist, taught at Syracuse University, and his daughter, Mary Becker, was also a professional violinist. Grandfather Becker, according to the family's oral history, had been the double-bass soloist for the German emperor. Lillian herself was considered a brilliant pianist and harpist. She was, for example, a harp soloist in the Grand Harp Orchestra of twelve harpists at the 1893 World's Fair in Chicago.[2]

On the Clark side of the family, Melville's father, George Clark, played the harp and melodeon and was known as an exceptional zither player. He also dealt in instruments, buying used ones and repairing them to resell. He even built melodeons, perfecting the reeds to a new

George W. Clark and Lillian Becker Clark, parents of Melville A. Clark. Photos probably taken before their marriage in 1880.

standard. (This small enterprise, which began in 1859 as the Clark Music Repair Shop, would become a business conglomerate: the Clark Music Company.) Around 1870 he organized the Clark Concert Company, composed of six members of the Becker and Clark families.[3] One of the players was his brother, also named Melville, on the flute. Brother Melville Clark (1850–1918) at the age of fourteen had enlisted at the Syracuse armory as a drummer boy in the 149th Regiment as it was setting out for the Civil War. After the war he returned to Syracuse, took a commercial course at Amos College, and became a bookkeeper for a local concern. However, the lure of music being stronger than his interest in journals and ledgers, he left to work for his brother George in the manufacture and repair of instruments (see chapter 2).[4]

George and Lillian had seven children: Arthur (b. 1881), Melville (b. 1883), Maude (b. 1885), Ernest (b. 1887), Bertha (b. 1891), and twins Grace and Clarence (b. 1895). They were all interested in music, and harp playing may have been the center of their musical interests.

Clark family in front of their home, around 1900. *Left to right, first row:* twins Clarence and Grace; *second row:* Melville, Bertha, George W., Maude, Ernest, Bertha Becker, and Arthur; *seated in rocker:* Lillian Clark.

The Clark children had the opportunity to play harps in ensemble, as there were always harps available for them from the Clark Music store's inventory. At various times the older children entertained on the concert harps, standing at the instruments because they were too small to reach the strings when seated. In Melville A. Clark's office hung a photo of four children: Arthur, Melville, Maude, and Ernest, their height progressions matched by their respective harps.[5]

George Clark apparently traveled to Illinois many weeks of the year, buying instruments and working on the Clark family enterprises, which included the manufacture of Story and Clark pianos as well as Apollo player pianos in Chicago and QRS piano rolls at the Clark Orchestra Roll Company in De Kalb, Illinois. During these absences, Arthur and Melville began to manage the family business. Ernest also

The Clark children at harps, around 1892. *Left to right:* Arthur, Melville, Maude, and Ernest.

worked in the Syracuse store for a while, but he too went west to become involved in the Clark family enterprises in Illinois. Bertha, Grace, and Maude worked in the store until they married and moved away from Syracuse. Maude became a professional harpist and played many musical programs with her brother Melville. Clarence was a bugler and dispatch runner in World War I, until his death in France in 1918 at the age of twenty-three.[6]

Melville was always interested in serious musical study and enjoyed spending time at the family store, trying out the various instruments, listening to other musicians play, and trying out new music to purchase. At a young age, he began to center his interests on the harp. As soon as he was tall enough to reach the strings of a concert harp, his father began to teach him to play. Melville's first formal lessons were with Van Veachton Rogers, a well-known harpist of his time. Rogers lived in Boston, summered in upstate New York, and regularly frequented the Clark Music store to purchase harp materials and music. Clark, in one of his recollections, stated, "I haven't the slightest intention of giving the impression that I was a boy wonder at the age of seven. I did play the harp fairly well. Perhaps it was my sincere love for music, together with the simplicity and forthrightness of youth that gave me the talent."[7]

Melville received his formal education from the Syracuse public schools. As a teenager he also began his travels outside his hometown, setting a lifetime pattern of constantly broadening his horizons. When Melville was between fifteen and sixteen, his father presented him with an Erard harp, which Melville brought on several short tours in North America. "My love for the harp was so great that [at age fourteen] I set about to try and build a small harp that could be carried in a large dress suit case of about two octaves which had no tones." This instrument served the purpose of a "practice harp" while en route on the train.[8] No doubt he traveled with older musicians who were friends of his father.

After high school he enrolled in music theory studies with Dr. William Berwald, instructor of harmony at Syracuse University, and Professor E. K. Winkler of Wells College in Aurora, New York, one-time teacher at Leipzig University in Germany.[9]

In 1905 Melville went to London to learn harp construction and to continue his studies of the concert harp (see chapter 3). While he was there, his father arranged for him to study harp with John Thomas of the Royal Conservatory of Music in London, who was harpist to the king of England, and with Aptommas, brother of John Thomas. Aptommas was said to have been a favorite harper at the court of Queen Victoria.[10] It was during this trip that Melville first saw the small Irish harps. When he returned from Europe, he began to design the small, portable Clark Irish Harp that became his most important contribution to the world of music.

All the years of studying and practicing served him well throughout his life. As a harpist, Clark had an active career, including more than four thousand appearances in America, Canada, and Europe.

Melville Clark in 1898 with an Erard harp, which was a present from his father.

Clark wrote: "After my return from studying abroad and after the completion of the design and construction of the Clark Irish Harp, I entered the concert field for a period. And it was my privilege to tour as assisting artist accompanist on the harp with such known personalities in the concert field as John McCormack, Mary Garden, Mme. Louise Homer, Nellie Melba, Alice Neilson and other great singing stars. During one of my concert tours, Margaret Wilson, daughter of our late President, heard me play and selected me as her assistant artist accompanist" (see chapter 8).[11]

Around 1919 William Place Jr., owner of a large music company in Providence, Rhode Island, began to rally a group of other harp enthusiasts to form a national harp group. Place was a mandolin player, and Mrs. Place was a well-known harpist in Providence. William enjoyed harp music, understood the instrument, and sold harps in his store. A provisional committee was established with Place as its secretary. He wrote to harpists all over the country, and in 1920 a harp convention was held in New York City. The result was the formation of the National Harp Association, with Carlos Salzedo as its first president. Maud Morgan was elected vice president, Alice Hills financial secretary, and Melville Clark treasurer. In just a few years there were eighteen chapters.

Each year a different chapter would host the National Harp Festival, which included an annual meeting and a formal concert program that always opened with a large national ensemble of harps. In 1932, when the twelfth festival took place in Syracuse, Salzedo conducted fifty-six concert harps through "Song of the Volga Boatmen," "Triptic Dance," and "Frére Jacques" in canon form in various registers.[12]

On January 8, 1921, the Clark family was united with another Syracuse musical family through the marriage of Melville Clark to Dorothy Speich. Her father, Andrew J. Speich, had also owned a music store in Syracuse and in Rochester, New York. After finishing high school, Dorothy studied piano for a year at the Boston Conservatory

An ensemble of fifty-six concert harps at the Twelfth Annual National Harp Festival held at the Lincoln Auditorium in Syracuse, April 16, 1932. *In foreground:* Carlos Salzedo, president and conductor; *second row:* Melville Clark, treasurer, and William Place Jr., founder; *extreme right:* Van Veachton Rogers, vice president.

of Music. In 1919 she was awarded the Morning Musical's piano scholarship to study with Adolph Frey at Syracuse University's Fine Arts Department. It was while she was playing in a recital at the College of Fine Arts that Melville first saw her and predicted a future for her in the musical world and perhaps in his personal world.[13] Dorothy and Melville were in many recitals and musicales together, before and during their marriage.

After the birth of their three children, Melville Jr. (b. 1921), Dorothy E. (b. 1923), and Timothy D. (b. 1925), the Clarks moved to the countryside from the city of Syracuse. In 1928 they purchased a farm in Oran, New York, near Cazenovia.[14] The main house was an important historic building known as the Travelers' and Drovers' Tavern. They restored the historic home to the period in which it was built, around 1820. Inside the house hung a framed proclamation from the Department of the Interior, which read as follows: "The Travelers' and Drovers' Tavern has been selected by the Historic and American Building Survey as possessing exceptional historic or architectural interest and as being worthy of most careful preservation for the benefit of future generations, and to this end a record of its present appearance and condition has been made and deposited for permanent reference in the Library of Congress."[15]

Before the railroads crossed upstate New York, it took drovers with their livestock eleven days to go the 250 miles from Buffalo to Albany, New York. The Travelers' and Drovers' Tavern was a stopover place for them. There were barns, corrals, feed for the livestock, and even a tar barrel to tar the feet of the turkeys so that they could walk on the gravel road. After reaching Albany, the animals were placed on barges and towed downriver to New York City to be sold.[16] In 2003 the present owners secured a listing for the former tavern and Clark home on the National Register of Historic Places.[17]

In her life in rural Oran, Mrs. Clark became a farmer and had the distinction of being one of the first women in the area to drive a tractor. All her life she studied music, but when she took up farming she laughed while telling about her strangely combined careers: "From the piano I've gone to potatoes."[18]

Clark family home, known as the Travelers' and Drovers' Tavern, Cherry Valley Turnpike, Oran, New York, 1934. Courtesy of Historical America Building Survey.

No ordinary farmer was Dorothy Clark. One day she was driving the tractor, and the next day she was gowned in a Paris frock ready to play for the president at the White House. Each summer she raised a thousand bushels of potatoes and cut more than a hundred tons of hay and alfalfa. She had thirty-five Nubian goats and a flock of more than five hundred chickens. Her aptitude for farming came, she thought, from her Swiss forebears. Her only training had been a weeklong course on farming at nearby Cornell University in Ithaca.[19]

Life was not just goats and potatoes at the Clark farm, for in the summer of 1935 Melville and Dorothy and the family driver, affectionately known as Ernie Groves, loaded up the three children, their musical instruments, and beach clothes and headed to Cape Cod. The ten-day "cruise" was made in what the Clarks called a Land Yacht, a commodious trailer outfitted to serve the needs of the family on the road. Melville Jr. remembers the trailer getting sideswiped by another car, but there was not enough damage to delay the trip to the ocean.[20]

The Clarks continued to perform together and singly through-out their married lives.[21] In 1939 Melville and Dorothy went on tour

Family trailer trip to Cape Cod, August 4, 1935. *In foreground:* Melville A. Clark with his harp; *left to right inside the trailer:* Melville Jr., Mrs. Dorothy Clark, young Dorothy Clark, and Timothy Clark. Courtesy of the *New York Times.*

in the New England area to promote the new electronic keyboard called the Novachord. A typical program began with Melville giving a description and a demonstration of antique and medieval instruments from his collection (see chapter 9). Then there would be a piece on the concert harp, followed by harp and Novachord duets, then Novachord solos by Dorothy, then more duets. The audience received a lesson in the history of musical instruments, including the latest one of that time, the Novachord.[22]

One often hears the phrase "business and pleasure will not mix." But in Melville Clark's case, it did not hold true. He loved his business life as much as his musical life. He was very active in the National Association of Music Merchants. In 1942 he was elected president of the ten thousand–member association. On the local level, he was a thirty-second-degree Mason and a charter member of the local Kiwanis chapter (1916) and the Syracuse Rotary International (1912), becoming president of each organization. In 1935 the American Legion awarded him its Good Citizen Medal.

Although Clark was primarily a harpist, he played twenty-seven instruments and even studied the cello longer than the harp.[23] In fact,

Clarks at home at the Travelers' and Drovers' Tavern, 1942. *Left to right:* Dr. Melville Clark Jr., Mr. and Mrs. Melville Clark, Dorothy Clark, and Timothy Clark, pictured in the music room. Courtesy of the *Syracuse Post-Standard*.

he played the whole Beethoven cycle of symphonies as a solo cellist with the Auburn Symphony Orchestra, which was privately owned by Thomas Mott Osborne, a nationally known prison reformer.[24] Despite being able to perform on so many instruments, he always preferred his harp and was never more than twenty-four hours without it. Even when he was on jury duty in 1929, he had a harp sent to the court-house. He traveled to many foreign countries, but never without his Irish Harp.[25]

Nevart Apikian, a reporter for the *Syracuse Post-Standard*, reflects back on her meetings with Melville Clark in the late 1940s and early 1950s: "Melville Clark was THE Clark Music Company. When I went for interviews, I remember him welcoming me with a warm smile. He always wore a custom made suit with subdued tie, the elegant

Melville Clark with Prescott cello around 1920.

gentleman. If he were discussing the Irish Harp, he often strummed a lovely melody as if his mission in life were to spread beautiful music. He was a pleasant interviewee and gave good quotes. I left with the upbeat feeling he inspired."[26]

On December 11, 1953, at the age of seventy, Melville Clark died suddenly of a heart attack while working at the Clark Music store. He was in the midst of many unfinished projects.[27]

Luther Cudworth, a reader from the Christian Science Mother Church in Boston, conducted Melville Clark's funeral service. It was Puritan in its simplicity, composed entirely of selections from the Bible and related passages from the writings of Mary Baker Eddy. There were several musical selections played to words written by Eddy, along with *In Paradisium* by DuBois and *Prayer* by Schubert.

To his friends, Clark was best known as a deeply religious man. The Clarks were devoted Christian Scientists, and Melville was a regular contributor to the *Christian Science Monitor*. A newspaper account of his death stated, "You never quite knew him unless you had seen him stand in a Christian Science meeting and give his testimony. There you had the key to his unfailing friendliness and quiet strength."[28]

The death of Melville Clark was a loss to the music world in general and to the harp world in particular. He started many musicians on their careers, either personally or through his development of the Clark Irish Harp. He was interested in all harpists, whether he actually knew them or not, and he followed their activities with interest.

Melville Clark Jr. had a marble stone erected on his father's grave in Oakwood-Morningside Cemetery, Syracuse, New York, with a fitting epitaph: "Concert Harpist, Author, Inventor of Clark Irish Harp, Founder of the Syracuse Symphony, President of Clark Music Company."

2

The House That Clark Built

PICTURE A SMALL STORAGE SHED with a window and a working door on a back street in a small city. Inside the shed sits a young man with his tools laid out before him, tinkering with a musical instrument that resembles a square piano. He calls it a melodeon.

The young man was George Waldo Clark, who went from being a tinkerer in a shed to the founder of a large musical enterprise that still exists today in upstate New York.

At the age of seventeen, George was working on a farm in Jamesville, New York, ten miles south of Syracuse, New York. He was, however, a fine harp and zither player, having played harp with the Cal Wagner Minstrels.[1] His father, a school principal in Marathon, New York, was also a fine harpist. In the 1850s George was dividing his time between farm chores and following his secret ambition: to invent and repair musical instruments. He combed the countryside in search of old, broken-down musical instruments to mend and rebuild. In the fall of 1858 George Clark left the farm with ten dollars in his pocket and walked to Syracuse to save the price of a rig. Unable to find work as an itinerant instrument repairman, a few months later in 1859 he opened the Clark Music Repair Shop.[2]

It was a humble beginning in a small, obscure storeroom on East Genesee Street, near the Hills Building, which stood on the former site of the Barton Opera House, in the vicinity of the State Tower Building. He began in a small way to repair musical instruments and to sell square pianos and organs. In 1860 he started building melodeons, sometimes referred to as reed organs, which were common in churches and homes in the late 1800s.[3] The melodeon's tone comes from one or more series of different-size reeds like the ones in an accordion or har-monica. Pressurized air, powered by the player pumping up and down on two pedals, passes over the reeds, producing the sound.

In the early 1860s the A. C. Chase Organ and Melodeon Company, located at South Salina and Fayette streets (known then as the Pike Block), hired Clark as one of their craftsmen.[4] On his own he began to experiment with ways of improving the melodeon's tonal quality as well as its all-around appearance, which tinkering caused him to lose his job. However, six months later Chase requested that George return at twice the salary, and, after the Civil War, Chase also hired George's brother Melville because "he had not been able in all America to find men to do such fine reed voicing." Together the brothers embarked on a program of tedious experimentation, tackling and solving many baffling challenges. Shortage of adequate tools and an almost complete lack of sufficient parts were two of their biggest problems. During the course of their work, they were successful in bending and shaping the reeds in a certain manner to produce an entirely different tone. This solution led to the first reed organ stop, a boon to the entire organ-manufacturing industry.[5]

In 1884 brother Melville teamed with Hampton L. Story in Chicago to become organ and piano manufacturers under the name of Story and Clark.[6] Melville continued to experiment and tinker with keyboard instruments. In 1901 he produced his first Apollo player piano, securing the patent in 1905. Seven years later, in 1912, he produced the first marking piano, which recorded live performances. The unusual recording of the machine could produce accurately every shade of expression and mannerism, preserving the tempo of the artist with every change as faithfully as phonograph records reproduce instrumental or vocal music.[7]

Meanwhile, in Syracuse, George Clark moved his fledgling business, now called the G. W. Clark Music Company, to 84 South Salina Street (later renumbered 352 South Salina Street). It was a little store, not much bigger than a storeroom, but it was located on the major thoroughfare of the growing city. Here he shared a storefront with the Krause Jewelry and Watch Repair Company.

Clark Music shared a storefront with Krause Jewelry on South
Salina Street, in Syracuse, around 1862.

Then came the Civil War. His son Melville A. Clark reminisced:

Father often related stories about his business during this period,
then he smiled when he mentioned the word "business," because
there wasn't any such thing. He installed a "notion counter" up
near the front of the store. He stocked it with all sorts of trinkets—
umbrellas, packets of pins and needles, toys and anything else that
could be sold for one price, 98 cents. The first business card read,

"G. W. Clark, Music and Fancy Goods." One day, F. W. Woolworth entered the store on a trip down from his home in Watertown, New York. He and George Clark discussed the idea of selling small articles at prices under one dollar. Many people have said that it was my father's notion counter from which the late Mr. Woolworth derived his idea for the 5¢ and 10¢ stores bearing his name.[8]

At the end of the war, George Clark discarded his notion-counter idea and returned to the music business. There were several years of hard times following the war, as the majority of people could not afford the luxury of a melodeon, organ, or harp. Slowly, the little shop began to regain solid ground and expenses were met, with even a few dollars of profit to show on the ledger after a week's operation.[9]

He remained in this location for more than thirty years, doing business without much fluctuation in sales. He had a good reputation for honesty in the music trades, but poor storekeeping skills. His displays were ordinary, and he was bashful in salesmanship. He had two employees. His youngest sister, Augusta Bond, was his bookkeeper and secretary, and Henry Norcross sold pianos and organs to country folks while George repaired instruments.[10]

In the early 1900s the Clark sons, Arthur and Melville, slowly assumed some of the management of the store. Despite the father's frequent trips to the family enterprises in Chicago and De Kalb, Illinois, the business in Syracuse had grown to such proportions that more spacious quarters were necessary. On November 15, 1905, Arthur and Melville purchased the Ginty Building at 416 South Salina Street. The building had six stories and was nicely situated only a block from the old store on one of the most traveled streets of Syracuse.[11]

George Clark wrote to his son Melville concerning the purchase of this large building: "I hardly know what to do about it. I did not mean you should buy the building at once, but get an option on it. Have you considered the cost and all the chances you have taken? It means a great deal of sacrifice on our part and self-denials. Now are you children ready to give up all self-pride and self-emulation? You and Arthur must put all your energy into the business. From now

George W. Clark poses with a newly acquired Grecian-style Erard harp, 1885.

on look out and deal directly with Mrs. Ginty [in purchasing the building]."[12]

The large store enabled the Clarks to expand the inventory and become the center of many new projects relating to music and entertainment. Melville, now twenty-three, took on the challenge of remodeling and equipping the store. He became the manager, and Arthur became the secretary and a director of the board. By May 1, 1907,

Clark's piano- and harp-moving wagon, 1904, at Jefferson and State streets, Syracuse.

Clark Music Company had incorporated and issued corporate stocks to the public with George W. Clark as its president.[13]

Arthur resigned both his positions in 1909. He went to work at the Rudolph Wurlitzer Company in New York City and later at the Jacob Doll Company, selling pianos. Arthur was not as interested in the music business as his father or brother and eventually went into the furniture business in California.[14]

After Clark Irish Harp production began in 1908 (see chapter 3), new space was needed to manufacture the harps and harp stands, called taborettes. Clark's Irish Harp design was an immediate success and prompted leasing an adjacent building in 1909. The board of directors voted to form a separate company to take care of the growing sales of the little harp. In 1911 the Clark Harp Manufacturing Company was established.[15]

The Clark Music Company business continued to grow, and by 1912 they had opened two branch stores in neighboring cities, Cortland and Watertown. Sales for the Clarks were lively in the preradio

Clark's newly purchased six-story music store, 416 South
Salina Street, Syracuse, 1907.

era, as there was a great need for pianos, melodeons, and smaller
instruments for people to play in their homes.

In 1919, at the urging of his eighty-year-old father, Melville purchased four hundred shares of company stock from his father with
a loan from the City Bank. This purchase made Melville the major
stockholder and brought him into control of the company. A new
board of directors was elected, with Melville as its new president.[16]

From the beginning it had not been the sole aim of the Clark
Music Company to sell musical instruments. Clark's was a company
that selflessly and consistently promoted music and music-related
activities in the area. In addition to keeping solvent, the objective of

the company was to advance the cause of music in the community, to devise ways and means for every child to have a musical education, and to aid talented musicians to become recognized by the public.[17]

On the business side of the ledger, "the house that Clark built" became much more than just a store with a counter selling music and instruments. The commercial operation was organized into departments, with staff appointments for working in the repair shop and for selling pianos, harps, sheet music, choral and instrumental music, musical instruments, player-piano rolls, and talking machines.[18] It was the largest and finest commercial musical establishment in central New York. It eventually became the seventh-largest music store in the United States. The company gained exclusive agencies for the sale of Steinway and Chickering pianos, as well as for Conn Band instruments and Stromberg-Carlson radios.[19]

The ticket sales department, called the Clark Musical Bureau, handled advance ticket sales for practically every traveling attraction that came to Syracuse, often handling them for nearby cities as well. It was possible to purchase a ticket at Clark's for anything from a piano recital to a reserve seat for the Ringling Brothers Barnum and Bailey Circus.[20]

Above the two sales floors, the third floor was a fine performing hall (Apollo Hall) with a capacity to seat three hundred persons. The acoustics were considered most favorable to musical programs. Art and music clubs could rent the hall for their exclusive use.[21] There was also a space dedicated to changing art exhibits of paintings and sculpture, decorated with potted palms and Oriental rugs.

In 1921 the store also served as the executive offices of the newly established Syracuse Symphony (see chapter 6). Melville Clark took on the monumental task of organizing the twelfth symphony in the United States. The first rehearsals were held on the third floor of the Clark store. The fledgling symphony held its board meetings in the Clark building, and its executive offices were maintained there for five years.[22]

The Onondaga Council of Girl Scouts also kept its office in the store for many years. Just before Clark's death in 1953, they gave him

The
George W. Clark Music House
A N N O U N C E S
T H E F O U R T H
Public Recital
Wednesday Evening, December 5, 1906

Please
Remove
Hats

Apollo Recital Hall, Clark Music Building
416-420 SOUTH SALINA STREET
SYRACUSE, : : : NEW YORK

Program from a recital in the Apollo Recital Hall of the Clark
Music Building, December 5, 1906.

a seldom-awarded certificate, a national citation in recognition of all
his kindnesses during the thirty years of their tenancy.[23]

Clark's interest spanned anything remotely related to music and
performance. In 1922 radio broadcasting came to Syracuse by a special wire, 130 miles away, from the WGY radio station in Schenectady,
New York. Melville Clark immediately embraced the new technology
and set up a small studio in his music store for instrumentalists to
broadcast musical performances, lectures, and interviews. He bought
advertising time to promote the Clark Music Company, an innovation
in radio's infancy. Later he became a promoter for the founding of
WSYR, Syracuse's first radio station, then a one hundred–watt channel. Many of the world's leading musicians who visited Syracuse were

introduced to the radio audience as guests on the Clark programs. When WSYR affiliated with NBC in 1932 and stepped up its power to one thousand watts, the Clark Music Company kept pace by building a large new broadcasting studio in its building and continuing to feed local programs with performances from the Clark studio.[24] Not surprisingly, Clark appeared as the honored guest on the first television broadcast in Syracuse when the station WHEN aired a two-hour program on December 1, 1948. He discussed his recent visit to London, played his harp, and displayed one of his prized music boxes from his collection.[25]

Building on the popularity of instrumental bands in the 1920s, the Clark Music Company in 1928 started a new marketing venture called the "Clark Plan," which was promoted throughout all the schools in New York State. Through this plan, students who signed up for band received a course of eight lessons from a certified teacher, an

A Clark Music Company broadcast over WSYR in Syracuse, direct from the store with harpist Jean Marie Brickman, 1932.

instruction book, and the instrument of choice—all for twelve dollars. In 1929 Stephen L. Carroll, a former clarinetist with the John Philip Sousa Band, was hired to manage this project. At the completion of the eight-lesson course, the entire band gave a demonstration concert. The parents were invited to hear the band, and then they could decide whether to buy an instrument. Seven of the twelve dollars would be applied toward the payment on the instrument, and there were ten months to pay the balance.

The Clark Plan then became available to organizations of every type, including the drum corps, Boy Scouts, orphans' homes, fire departments, American Legion posts, the New York State Railway Band, and American veteran groups. There was even a Ukrainian string band made up of guitars, harps, and seventy-five mandolins. More than 125 such organizations were formed under the Clark Plan. Musicians, music educators, students, and parents embraced this generous and innovative arrangement.[26]

Melville A. Clark was a fine entrepreneur as well as a dedicated musician. During the Depression in the 1930s, 80 percent of the music and piano companies in the United States went out of business. The Clarks survived when they diversified by selling "white goods," such as refrigerators and electric stoves, next door to their music store.[27]

The Clark Music Company's techniques for selling products seemed aggressive in the first quarter of the twentieth century, when companies had little or no money for advertising. Melville believed in spending money to promote the company's goods and services. The company made extensive use of direct mail advertising, not a common practice at the time, and any musical event in New York State carried a Clark's ad in its program. They advertised in all major national musical magazines as well as the music dealers' publications. They bought time in early radio and published *Hall O'Harps Monthly,* a nationally distributed newsletter that was free to harpists.

During the late 1920s and 1930s Clark's attracted shoppers to the store windows at Christmastime by showcasing young harpers playing carols on Clark Irish Harps and piping the music out to the shoppers on the street.[28] One harper remembers playing her Clark Harp in the

Newsletter, *Hall O'Harps Monthly,* July 1919.

store windows on Saturday mornings during the school year. She and her sister took turns sitting in the solo window spot, and at the end of the morning they each received an envelope with a crisp one-dollar bill inside.[29]

A further marketing device to bring in additional sales was to use the company's own labor force to get prospective clients into the store. Anyone who suggested the name of a prospect received a commission when the sale was made. This device not only increased sales but also became an important benefit to employees, numbering seventy-five people during the peak seasons. The approach of involving every employee, whether bookkeeper, office boy, carter, or technician, was quite innovative for the time.

During an interview for an article in the *National Music Trade Review* in 1929, Clark was asked how the company had developed, held, and expanded its business over a long period of years to bring it to its present state. His explanation was simple: "There are three phases in successful merchandising. . . . First, create a desire for good music. Second, advertise and tell folks you supply the music. Third, sell them only the best quality goods. Then hire good help and pay them well for the sales they produce."[30]

Clark was a lifelong promoter of business, music, education, and himself.[31] He continued to expand the business well into his sixties. In 1946 he purchased Wurlitzer's entire harp-making equipment inventory from the factory in Tonawanda, New York. Rudolph Wurlitzer wrote to Clark telling him of their expansion in the organ business, which would require more space in their plant.

The letter went on to say that they intended to close out their entire stock of harps and harp parts. The next day, following the receipt of this letter, Clark took a plane to Tonawanda to have a look. He purchased the major part of the stock, consisting of twenty-five harps in the last stages of completion.[32] He described his grand buy-out to Carlos Salzedo, president of the National Harp Association, as a wonderful opportunity for the business.[33] Clark wrote, "We purchased all the dies, jigs, drawings, etc. 11 tons of it from the Wurlitzer Company and took their two best harp makers. We brought them to Syracuse and just turned out our first new instrument and it is a 'joy.' We will be able to make 25 of these [pedal] harps with the material we have on hand."[34] This purchase put Clark's in the concert harp–manufacturing business, whereas previously the company had turned out only the small Clark Irish Harps. The new harps were called the Melville Clark Pedal Harps.

The standard wooden "A" model had not been built since 1948. It was more profitable to rebuild the standard A models to the specifications of the Baby Grand Model with the extended soundboards and structural improvements. Clark said he could rebuild a harp in one week that would last forty years.[35]

From the beginning, the Clark Music Company was a family business. Executive officers on the board were Clarks, and the younger family members were employed in various departments and the repair shop. During World War II Dorothy S. Clark stepped in to manage the sheet music and phonograph departments, putting aside her piano-teaching career. After Melville Clark's death in 1953, his widow became the manager and president of the company. The younger son, Timothy, was appointed assistant manager.[36]

Without Melville Clark the Clark Harp Manufacturing Company continued to produce the full concert-size Melville Clark Pedal Harps for only a brief time, under the supervision of Eric Hildebrandt and Otto Volkman, former Wurlitzer harp builders.[37] Since Mrs. Clark was not interested in the harp-manufacturing and -repair aspect of the business, she sold the entire lot to Eric Hildebrandt for twenty-five hundred dollars on June 9, 1954, so that he could make harps out of his home at 609 Almond Street. The contract specified the sale of machinery, jigs, dies, special tools, storage bins, and raw material. Not to be sold were the harp strings and the patents held by the Clark Harp Company. Hildebrandt had thirty days to remove all said items. To facilitate the move, the contract stated that the Clark Company would deliver the entire purchase of materials to any location within the limits of the city of Syracuse without charge.[38]

The very large and extensively equipped harp-repair shop was also closed six months after Clark's death, probably for financial reasons. So, with the stroke of a pen, ninety-five years of harp repair, design, and construction ended for the House of Clark.

In 1960 the company was sold to Guido Singer and Jack Solovei. In a separate purchase the new owners acquired the Clark Music Company name and history for ten thousand dollars. In 1965 Sibley's Department Store of Rochester bought the 416 South Salina Street property to erect a large four-story branch store on South Salina and West Jefferson streets.[39] The Clark Music Company then relocated to the city's outskirts. It remains a viable music business today, currently owned by Hugh Murphy Sr. The inventory reflects the needs of clients of the twenty-first century, with the emphasis on the sale of pianos, electric keyboard instruments, audiovisual components, and sound equipment. The Clark Music Company is still the exclusive agent for sales and repair of Steinway pianos in central New York and in Albany, where a branch of the company serves the Capital District.[40] The ads for the music company always state, "in business since 1859."

The house that Clark built is one of the nation's oldest continuously operated music establishments. The house was built with good foundations and brought the Clark name to eminence culturally and commercially. The company has survived two world wars, the Great Depression, four landlords, and a major relocation.

3

The Clark Irish Harp

THE HARP WAS TOO BIG and the boy was too small when five-year-old Melville Clark began playing. He received his first lessons from his father, George W. Clark, a gifted musician and instrument maker. As a young boy Clark was featured on many musical programs in and around Syracuse. He always played on a large concert pedal harp from the family's music store. To reach the strings on the concert harp, he was obliged to play standing up and later recollected, "Somehow it seemed to me that I just wouldn't ever grow tall enough so I could sit and play like a regular harpist."[1] He once wrote:

> I so frequently was met with the statement by people that they loved the music of the harp and wished that they could play, but expressed their inability to do so because of the cost of the concert harp. I recall very vividly a visit to my father's store, where there was a display of violins, pianos, harps, drums and other instruments. While there, a gentleman most prominent in business, Mr. L. C. Smith, President of the [L. C. Smith and Brothers] typewriter company, came in and asked the price of a concert harp. When he was told the price was $1,000, he was apparently astonished that the cost was so high. Then he walked to the door and suddenly turned to my father and said, "I certainly would not invest that much money to find out if my daughter could learn to play." The refusal of this man to be willing to pay a sum of $1,000 for a harp made a deep impression on me. But at the time I did not give thought as to how this objection could be overcome.[2]

All of Melville Clark's early education took place in Syracuse while he lived at home with his family. After Clark completed high school, he attended Central City Business Institute while working as a manager in the family store. According to Clark's biographical statements, he enrolled at Syracuse University for a course in music harmony. After the completion of this course, his father decided that Melville should go abroad to continue his studies in music and learn basic harp construction.[3]

Thus, young Melville sailed to London in 1905 to study harp construction in the world-renowned Erard harp factory. The Clark Music Company was the exclusive agent for Erard harps in the United States.[4] For a half century, 1810 to 1860, Erards were the most important harps being made in the world. Before Sebastian Erard perfected the pedal mechanism in 1810, only the medieval harp was available.[5]

The medieval harp was a simple diatonic instrument, and when modern instrumental music arose, that harp's limits were too narrow to accommodate it. Even though its tone was charming, the medieval harp almost fell into oblivion. It had but one scale, and the only way to obtain an accidental was to shorten the string as much as needed by firmly pressing it with the finger. This situation was very unsatisfactory, because it temporarily left the harpist with only one hand for playing. For this reason, we do not find the harp featured in early symphonic scores. Until the early nineteenth century composers used it mainly for the sake of its historical character.

About 1720 the first step toward the construction of a concert, or pedal, harp was taken. One person after another added a little to the process, until Erard perfected the pedal mechanism, making the pedal harp a fully chromatic instrument. The pedal harp has seven pedals, one for each note: C, D, E, F, G, A, and B. The left foot controls three of the pedals; the right foot controls the remaining four. When the harpist steps on the pedals, the pedal discs located on the neck of the harp are altered, and the strings are lengthened or shortened. Thus, natural, sharp, and flat notes are produced. In each position the pedal can be secured in a notch so that the foot does not have to keep holding it in the correct position.

This mechanical improvement naturally led to a much wider use of the instrument. Meyerbeer and Wagner began to use it extensively in their operas, and Berlioz introduced the harp into symphonic music of the romantic school. However, the modern concert harp, with its intricate pedal mechanism, was prohibitively expensive for all but very few.

Clark's apprenticeship at the Erard factory was under the guidance of the capable and highly regarded Mr. Adlington, superintendent of the Erard factory. During Clark's stay in London, he took harp lessons with John Thomas, harpist to the king of England. Clark stated, "I not only was taught the rudiments of harp construction and designing, to the most minute details, but I was also shown the very latest technique in harp playing. I believe this was the first time a harp player also became a harp maker." Thomas advised Clark to study in Paris with the famous French teacher Alphonse Hasselmans before returning to the United States.[6] Clark wrote:

> I was in love with Paris immediately, and [after a few weeks] it was with reluctance that I boarded the boat train to return to England, as I had promised I would see John Thomas on the way back to America. Cutting my return stay in England short, I took a boat to Dublin in order to gain firsthand information about the famous harps of Ireland. I learned much of the romantic part the instrument has played in that country's history. It was while doing so that the idea of developing a small harp was something I wanted to do. Maybe I was remembering how I had to stand up to play the concert harp as a child.[7]

In Ireland Clark visited Cardinal Logue, primate of Ireland, whom he had met on the steamer from the United States. "After a week of frequent chats we had an animated conversation about harps, especially the Irish harp. Noting my great interest and enthusiasm for them, he invited me to visit him in Queenstown [Cobh] so that he could show me his Irish harp, which he cherished exceedingly."[8] He liked the cardinal's Irish harp and stated, "I sought one like it and I managed to buy several of the Irish made instruments [to bring back to America], which probably introduced the Irish harp idea in this country." The famous poet and composer Thomas Moore had owned one of the harps.[9] Clark reminisced, "I returned home on the fastest boat possible and began drawing plans and designing my small harp." Clark's goal was to design and build a harp that was affordable for many people, small enough for children to play, and light enough to be easily portable.[10]

Of his eventual design Clark wrote, "The Clark Irish Harp is built after the model owned by Thomas Moore, preserving some of the characteristics of size, shape, and construction."[11] Roslyn Rensch states in her book *Harps and Harpists,* "Clark harps, particularly in their soundbox construction, followed the design of the small Egan harp, rather than that of the earlier 'true' Irish harp."[12]

The historic harps that Clark had seen in Ireland were made of bog oak. Because bog oak was unavailable in the United States, he made his harps of easily obtainable rock maple. The early Clark Irish Harps were made by hand, with Clark probably perfecting the design as he produced each one.

Clark began numbering his early harps with no. 101. An early model, no. 134, survives (it is currently owned by Patricia DeBottis of Nelson, New York). This harp, still being played today, predates all the patents Clark subsequently obtained. The complete provenance of the instrument is unknown; it is known, however, that it was made to be given as a prize, most likely in 1908 or 1909.

This early Clark Harp was designed for an adult or child to play standing. With the harp attached to the stand, it is too high to be tipped back for playing. Unbolted and removed from the stand and resting on the floor, it is a harp that a younger child could play. While writing about the evolution of the design of his Irish Harp, Clark noted, "One of the greatest difficulties was to place the harp upon a base that would give the same posture when played as that of a concert harp and yet have firmness on the floor so that some vigorous player would not cause the harp to move and thus throw them out of their playing position."[13] He later solved this functional problem with the design of the taborette, a four-legged base on which to attach the harp. (For further details, see the section on harp construction at the end of this chapter.)

Melville Clark, 1909, playing an early model of his harp,
which was bolted to a stand.

The harp design that became the standard Clark Irish Harp went
into production around 1911. It was beautifully designed, with careful attention to detail. Clark stated that the construction of one harp
required 168 parts and six different woods.[14]

The harps were available with maple-wood finishes in either a
transparent green or a natural wood color. The four feet on the Clark
Irish Harp were carved to look like the feet of an Irish wolfhound,
each foot having three toes. Gilt decorations appear in a shamrock

pattern along the borders of the harp's neck, pillar, and body.[15] The artwork on the soundboard consists of a fourteenth-century Celtic green-and-gold medallion design and two interlaced wolfhound designs. The medallions are characters representing the letters *B* and *D* (which seem to be merely decorative). At the top of the letters is a figure of a head showing the Norwegian influence on Irish art of the fourteenth century.

The standard harp has thirty-one strings. Each string has a blade, or "finger," at the top, which can raise the pitch a halftone when rotated a quarter turn. Each blade is stamped with the name of its corresponding string.[16] With the use of these blades, the harp can be played in all the major keys and relative minor keys without retuning. The blades permit occasional accidentals during the course of playing; they gave the twentieth-century Irish harp player much greater choice of key than ever before.[17]

Clark was granted eight patents for the design of his harp (see the table of patents at the end of this chapter). He designed the harps in two sizes. The A model with thirty-one strings was thirty-nine inches high and weighed twelve pounds. The B Junior model had twenty-six strings, was twenty-five inches high, and weighed six pounds. He was also granted two more U.S. patents for the design of the taborette for the A model, to protect the ingenious features from being copied.

Clark was eager to introduce his Irish Harp to the public. He launched a vigorous campaign to promote the idea of a small, affordable instrument. The Clark Music Company began selling the early-model Clark Irish Harp around 1909 to beginning harpers and music teachers. The basic outfit included the Clark Irish Harp, adjustable base (which preceded the taborette), tuning key, pitch pipe, and a cambric cover. This package cost $125 for the thirty-one-string harp. The smaller harp of twenty-six strings, which he named the MAC Jr., cost $75 for the basic outfit. Clark also offered other accessories, such as an instruction book, instruction course, waterproof carrying cover, padded traveling trunk, harp-string gauge, tuning fork, strings, string case, music, and a shoulder strap to suspend the harp from the shoulder while playing in a standing position.[18]

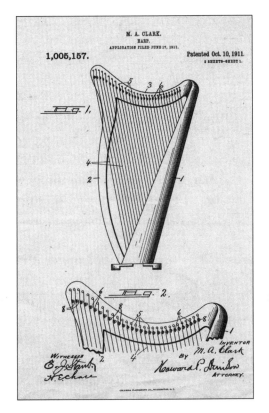

Clark Irish Harp patent drawing for adjustable bridge pins and frets, 1911.

The self-instruction course published in 1910 by the Clark Music Company (*Instructions for Playing the Harp* lesson synopsis) was prepared specifically for Clark Irish Harp beginners. For harp students who were unable to find a teacher, Clark's also published a course of lessons. There were twenty photos in which Van Veachton Rogers, an internationally renowned harpist and teacher, demonstrated proper technique. Clark specified that the paper be American-made "French-Japan Paper," buff in color, measuring 13¾ x 10⅛ inches. It sold for $2.[19]

From 1909 to 1918 the Clark Music Company also published a line of harp compositions, specifically composed for the Clark Irish Harp by Van Veachton Rogers. "Waltz Albania," "Wooden Shoe Dance," "Lullaby," "Petite Etude," and "March of the Marionettes" were some of the most popular pieces.

In 1932 Clark expanded on the first instruction book to a full *Play the Harp* edition of one hundred pages. This book, written for both lever- and pedal-harp students, was published by Schirmer in New York and Theodore Presser in Philadelphia. It sold for $2.50.[20]

The company leased a four-story building behind the Clark Music Company's Salina Street store in 1909 to be the site for manufacturing the new harps.[21] This building fronted on the 400 block of South Clinton Street, so "the house that Clark built" now extended from Salina Street to Clinton Street. So many sales resulted from this new instrument that in 1911 the directors of the Clark Music Company voted to create a separate company called the Clark Harp Manufacturing Company.[22]

While promoting his new harp, Clark organized a harp orchestra to include all beginning students, as well as advanced harpers. The Clark Irish Harp made its first formal appearance in Lincoln Hall (Auditorium) of Central High School in Syracuse on March 18, 1910. Twenty-three harpists played the harps on the program—the first harp band in the country. Clark's aunt Bertha E. Becker, also a harpist, conducted the orchestra. Clark played several Irish and Scottish airs as solos on the new instrument to demonstrate that a small harp could fill a large auditorium with lovely music.[23]

On June 30, 1910, the twenty-three harps and twenty-six violins performed Handel's "Largo" before the New York State Music Teachers Association at Crouse College of Syracuse University. Clark demonstrated to all the teachers present that children and people with no previous musical knowledge could become proficient for orchestra playing in less time with the Clark Irish Harp than with any other refined instrument. He wrote, "The formation of the first Irish Harp Band in the Country was due to the improvements on the new harp."[24]

Once the public began hearing the Clark Irish Harp, the harp sold itself. Clark wrote to a friend in 1911, "Wanamaker, Ditsons and Carl Fischer are all taking on the little harp [to sell] in New York City."[25] That same year the Clark Harp won the Silver Medal from the Turin, Italy, Exposition for developing the finest portable harp ever invented.

The following year, Wurlitzer began advertising the harp in its wholesale and retail catalogs. The company ordered a large number of Clark Harps to supply its customers. At the time, Wurlitzer was a large, dependable international source for musical instruments and accessories.[26]

By 1912 the Clark Harp Manufacturing Company was making thirty-five harps every month, but the company could not keep pace with orders and negotiated with the Lyon and Healy Harp Company of Chicago to make 250 Clark Irish Harps: the A model, for $42.50 each with a royalty of $6.38, and the B model, for $27.00 with a royalty of $4.05.[27] Clark personally guaranteed payment for this transaction with Paul J. Healy. The added name of Lyon and Healy appears only on instruments that were intended for their trade or sales.[28]

Lyon and Healy were great Clark Harp enthusiasts. After Clark visited the factory showroom in 1916, he wrote to Van Veachton Rogers, "Lyon and Healy is quite stirred up over the Clark Irish Harp. They have a separate room for displaying them and have assigned a Mr. Crayson to devote his time to selling them in Chicago."[29]

An updated three-year contract between the Clark Harp Manufacturing Company and Lyon and Healy became effective January 1, 1917. The new production cost to the Clarks was $54.54 for the A models and $32.00 for the B models. The royalties were increased to $9.50 and $5.76, respectively.[30]

Lyon and Healy continued making the Clark Irish Harp for many years until 1935, when the Clark Manufacturing Company in Syracuse bought back the harp patterns, jigs, dies, and parts. Mr. Keenly, manager of the harp department, wrote that Lyon and Healy was very far behind in the production of its own concert pedal harps but needed more Clark Irish Harps to sell immediately.[31]

Melville Clark set up the first sales agreement as early as July 1, 1911. Any musical instrument dealer or music teacher could use it to sell the Clark Irish Harps, lessons by mail, and accessories. It was called the "Special 50 and 2% Jobber's Agreement." The dealer, or jobber, received a 50 percent discount and 2 percent more if he paid cash in ten days. To qualify, a dealer had to buy at least $500 worth of goods in

RETURN THIS COPY

| Special 50 and 2% Jobber's Agreement
Terms and Conditions of Sale. | | Revised to July 1st, 1911 |

C-1

AGREEMENT
— FOR THE —
UNITED STATES OF AMERICA

In force between Jobbers of "Melville A. Clark" and "Mac Irish" Harps, Accessories and Lessons by Mail, and

MELVILLE A. CLARK
OF SYRACUSE, N. Y., U. S. A.

(Subject to Change and Revision on notice from Melville A. Clark or His Assigns)

For the respective Prices and Terms upon said goods, reference must be made to the latest list, separately issued.

Any jobber desiring to handle Melville A. Clark or Mac Irish Harps, Accessories and Lessons by Mail and receive the 50 and 2% discount must purchase at one time, in one shipment, at least $500 worth of said goods, figured at the 50 and 2% cost prices, for each and every store to which he wishes to sell said goods. In addition, the dealer must have an established place of business suitable to the display of such goods and agree at all times to carry in stock a representative line and purchase during the year an amount of goods sufficiently satisfactory in the estimation of the manufacturer to warrant a continuation of this special discount.

In consideration of receiving the discount as provided for in this agreement on such goods,_____hereby agree to purchase of the manufacturer, Melville A. Clark or his assigns, the said goods on the following terms and conditions:—

1. That_____will not sell or offer to sell at retail, either directly or indirectly, any of the said goods which are patented or copyrighted at a lower price than indicated, respectively, in the printed list furnished, and to be furnished, by the manufacturer from time to time, except as provided in Paragraph 8 of this instrument.

2. That_____will sell only to such retailers as have signed and filed with the manufacturer the retail dealer's agreement.

3. That the manufacturer will replace, free of charge, through his distributors, any broken or defective parts whenever the breakage or defectiveness is traceable to causes governed by the manufacturer, and will repair within a reasonable time after shipment, without charge, at the factory, any inherently defective goods, providing transportation charges are prepaid. Dealers and distributors are not authorized to make repairs at the expense of the manufacturer.

4. That no license or permission is granted for the alteration of any part of, or any addition to, any of said goods protected by letters patent or copyright, or for the substitution of any of said goods or a part not made by Melville A. Clark or his assigns, and all of said goods must be sold and delivered exactly as catalogued by the manufacturer.

5. That the labels and plates of said goods must not be removed or defaced.

6. That the discounts quoted to dealers apply only to the sale of said goods to users in the United States of America, and it is distinctly understood that this agreement grants no exclusive agency or territory.

7. That the manufacturer shall have the right and reserves unto himself the right to terminate this agreement at any time, notice of termination of said agreement to be forwarded by mail in writing by the manufacturer to the last known address of the party or parties signing this agreement, the termination and annulment of said agreement to take effect at once.

8. That_____agree to pay for said goods the printed prices established from time to time by the manufacturer, less the discounts of 50 and 2% for cash in ten days, 30 days net (except Styles O Jr. and A-1), and to sell said goods as hereinbefore provided, except that it is understood a discount not greater than 10% may be allowed to bona fide professional users and teachers of *said* harps. Also that_____will not give, present or otherwise include gratis anything valuable in the price of said goods catalogued by said manufacturer, nor any other merchandise, trading stamps or other inducement as an incentive to promote their sale; that_____will give no commission on sale of said goods in any form, except as hereinbefore provided, and except in lieu of a regular salary to salesmen whose services are employed regularly and exclusively.

9. That_____agree to change said retail prices from time to time to meet and conform to the manufacturer's retail list, it being understood that at least thirty days notice of such change shall be mailed by the manufacturer and that all changes shall be uniform to all dealers throughout the country.

10. That_____agree, after notification by said manufacturer, not to sell or exchange said goods to infringers of the letters patent or copyright applied for, issued, or to be issued, under which said goods are manufactured or published, or to be manufactured or published, or who have violated the agreement to sell said goods at full list prices established by said manufacturer.

11. That it is understood that United States and foreign copyrights have been issued for said Lessons by Mail, and letters patent have been applied for, and many claims allowed for, patents on parts of said harps, designs, and certain of the accessories.

12. That this agreement is to take the place of any prior existing agreement between the parties bearing upon the subject matter as covered in, or provided by, this agreement.

13. That this agreement is personal to the party signing same, and is not transferable or assignable without the written consent of the manufacturer. Also that said Clark may assign this agreement to an individual, firm or corporation, which shall manufacture, publish and deal in said goods.

14. That harps are furnished with tuning key, pitch pipe or fork, complete course of lessons by mail, high-low base (except Mac Lug Irish Harp, which is supplied with body brace and sling, and Style O Jr.), independent lever action, nickel plated tuning pins, ebony bridge pins, felt padded feet.

Dated at_____this_____day of	Jobber's Signature_____[L. S.]
_____191__	Street and Number_____
Witness to Jobber's Signature:	City_____State_____
_____	
Accepted this_____day of_____191__	
Manufacturer's Signature_____	

Jobber's Agreement to sell the Clark Irish Harp, 1911.

one shipment. He also needed to have an established place of business suitable to display a representative line of Clark Harps and accessories.

Professor Van Veachton Rogers became the first traveling salesman for the new instrument. At each prospective client's school or music store, Rogers arranged to give a short concert on the new harp. Before the arrival of the audience, a small circular to promote the instrument was placed on every seat. After each concert he invited discussions and handed out additional promotional literature.[32] Rogers wrote to Clark, his former pupil, in 1912:

> We need someone to promote the way in fundamental [harp] work until the harpists and teachers wake up to the fact of the importance of the Clark Irish Harp as a necessity for the development of touch, tone and technique. The course that I am taking with the instrument is first playing it and showing its beautiful qualities and possibilities. Next in line, proving without question its great advantages for the development of fundamental principles and its necessity to the beginner from many standpoints. The little harp is getting to be a serious subject with me.[33]

According to an agreement dated September 9, 1912, Professor Rogers received $600 annually, plus expenses, for his services in selling and popularizing the instruments. His picture appears in the original harp instruction book, showing proper seating position at the harp and hand positions on the strings for beginning harpists.[34]

Rogers went on tour with entertainer Charles Grilley as part of the Red Path Chautauqua Circuit, from June to September in 1913 and again in 1914. Rogers wrote, "We have short jumps of two or three days in a place, and the advantages are going to be splendid for doing some excellent work [promoting the Clark Irish Harp]."[35] In the summer of 1913 the circuit traveled to Ohio, Indiana, Michigan, Wisconsin, Illinois, Kansas, Oklahoma, Nebraska, Iowa, Pennsylvania, West Virginia, and Missouri. They performed the following year in North and South Dakotas, Iowa, and Missouri. This full schedule gave Rogers a tremendous opportunity to play and promote sales of the harp in America's heartland.[36]

Professor Van Veachton Rogers demonstrating proper placement of the left hand for an instruction book, 1910.

Melville Clark himself undertook several tours promoting the Clark Irish Harp. In 1910 he advertised his harp in New York City at the Waldorf-Astoria for the International Art Society of New York City, at the Astor Hotel for the Century Theatre Club, at Wanamaker's Department Store, and in a concert for the Victor Talking Machine Company (later RCA).[37]

By 1911 the Clark Irish Harp was in production, and Clark enthusiastically promoted the new instrument on the following tours:

• 1912 Midwest tour: Flint and Bay City, Michigan; Cincinnati; and Chicago

• 1914 Midwest tour: Detroit and Grand Rapids, Michigan, with John McCormack (tenor)

• 1915–16 tour: New Hampshire, New York, and Pennsylvania with Margaret Wilson

• 1918 tour of World War I soldier camps: accompanying Margaret Wilson with Clark Irish Harp for three weeks in cantonments from Camp Merritt to Camp May, New Jersey

• 1919 tour: Milwaukee; Denver; Kansas City, Missouri; San Francisco; Toronto; and Ottawa, Canada

In a March 27, 1914, recital Melville Clark played at the White House for the first time. J. Russell Paine, general manager of Clark Music Company, wrote to Professor Rogers, "Melville played the Lyon and Healy 22 in the White House for the President [Wilson] and the elite of Washington yesterday at a special musicale. He introduced the Irish Harp as well."[38] (See chapter 8.)

Musicians and educators internationally endorsed the little harp from Syracuse. Dr. Maria Montessori of Rome, Italy, said, "The small harp has a complete scale and simplicity." She preferred the stringed instrument because a teacher could play it facing the children while singing. It was used in the classrooms as the guitar and autoharp are used today.[39]

Some of the first schools in New York State to purchase a Clark Irish Harp for their music departments were the Emma Willard School in Troy, the State Normal School in Potsdam, the Immaculate Heart Academy in Watertown, and Cornell University.[40]

In 1918 the Clark Music Company began publishing a national harp-related newsletter, the *Hall O'Harps Monthly*, with no advertising. It featured poetry, meeting notices, concert programs, biographical profiles of harpists, and photos of adults and children performing on pedal harps or their Clark Irish Harps.[41]

The *Crescendo* was a national monthly music magazine (published on Tremont Street in Boston) devoted exclusively to the interests of harp, mandolin, guitar, ukulele, and steel guitar. In 1916 its harp editor, A. Francis Pinto, wrote a column extolling the virtues of the Clark Irish Harp, citing its portability, low cost, good size for children, and the ease of organizing a large class of children to study the Irish harp.

Pinto said, "I believe that intelligent teaching of the Clark Irish Harp, later applied to the concert harp, would result in placing more harpists on the concert stage side by side with the distinguished pianists, organists, violinists, and cellists of the present day."[42]

Soon after the harp went into production, some distinguished people purchased one for themselves: composer Victor Herbert, Lady Eaton of Toronto, and John McCormack, renowned opera tenor and concert singer of Irish songs, who bought one for his children. The Trasks of Saratoga Springs, New York, owners of Yaddo (now an international artists' retreat), bought three—one for themselves and two for special gifts. One of the recipients was Thomas Mott Osborne, a famous American prison reformer of the early 1900s.[43]

Even after hundreds of Clark Irish Harps had been produced and sold, Clark continued to experiment with many adaptations. Some new ideas were decorative, and some pertained to mechanical changes. One of his ideas was to customize the harp's decorative features. A memo in the Clark Papers, dated April 30, 1917, presents an ambitious idea: "to manufacture the Clark Spanish Harp, Clark Florida Harp, Clark Russian Harp, Clark Italian Harp, Clark French Harp, Clark Japanese Harp, Clark American Harp, Clark Hawaiian Harp, these harps to be done in a suitable finish to match the general decoration scheme of the different nations, according to their best and most popular art."[44]

In 1919 Clark designed a model "D" prototype, with a thumb action made of clear glass. It had thirty-four strings, and the upper tuning pins were made of aluminum.[45] By 1931 the thumb action was improved to operate on either side of the neck. This harp sold for $295.[46] However, this model did not become popular, as it was difficult to construct, and it was not practical to use the thumb for sharping a string.

Clark received a patent in 1920 for a means to change the pitch of multiple strings simultaneously with one movement of the hand, in the same manner as the feet operate the change of pitch in the pedal harp. He devised a way to link the octaves in unison to one dital, or finger piece. He called it "gang tuning." Activation of the gang tuning could be accomplished by hand under the neck with the left hand, behind the neck with the right hand, or at the pillar through links, depending on how the finished instrument was designed.[47] Because Clark made his portable harps available at a reasonable cost, this additional complicated, and therefore costly, mechanism did not become a realistic addition to the A model Irish Harp.

A variation of the gang-tuning patent was another Irish Harp improvement relating to the hand mechanism for raising and lowering the pitch of a set of strings. Clark filed for this patent for what he called the "Trench Harp" in January 1919 and received it three years later. The improvements he made enabled a player to raise the pitch of multiple strings at least two halftones above their normal pitch. The movable frets could be operated by hand from either side of the neck of the harp. A locking device automatically locked frets in the desired positions. Clark made the handles partially luminous to make the harp playable at night around a campfire or in other minimally lit areas.[48] Perhaps Melville Clark had been inspired to design the Trench Harp model shortly after World War I, as he had been active during the war entertaining the troops in several military camps.

In the late 1940s Clark developed a relatively successful new harp model, the Clark Baby Grand Harp. It differed from the A model in that it had an extended soundboard fourteen inches wide; it stood fifty-two inches high, including the taborette, and weighed fourteen pounds. It was strung with Clark Nylon Harp Strings and sold for $325. Later, "Visualite" (see chapter 5), a crack-preventive finish Clark invented, was added to the soundboard. The price of the Baby Grand model with this added feature in 1950 was $425.[49]

In the concerted efforts of manufacturing and promoting the new Baby Grand Harp model, fewer and fewer of the standard A models were made. During World War II people were not as concerned with purchasing musical instruments. The workshop would gear up from time to time and produce a few new ones, but generally clients were encouraged to buy the new Baby Grand model or earlier A models that had been rebuilt, using nylon strings, and the wider soundboard with the Visualite finish.

At the close of World War II, when synthetic materials became more plentiful for commercial use, Clark began to work on his all-plastic (fiberglass) harp idea. He produced a few using the design of the Baby Grand, but the results were a poor second compared to the quality of the wooden harps. Therefore, he went on to design a smaller harp with five fewer strings. Producing the body of the harp was his main problem. In a letter to a fellow harpist, Clark wrote a discouraging report: "We are still trying to master the problem of our molds for the plastic-fiberglass harp. We have three sets of them, because each time something was not just right."[50] From 1950 to 1953 Clark worked with both the Atlas Plastics Company of Buffalo and Lunn Laminates of Glen Cove, New York, to produce a body shell for the twenty-six-string harp.[51]

Each model they made was unsatisfactory to him because each had dimensions that differed slightly from the original design; if the length of the sounding board was not precisely according to the specifications, the entire instrument could become distorted.[52] Clark spent his last eight years working on this project, the "Timothy Clark Plastic Harp."[53]

The fiberglass harp became the best publicized of all the harps, however, when Elaine Vito, harpist for the NBC Orchestra, appeared in the December 13, 1948, issue of *Life* playing the fiberglass harp underwater. This same photo appeared on the cover of the 2001 winter issue of the *International Folk Harp Journal*. Besides exposure in the print media, the Clark Irish Harp appeared in the 1946 Hollywood film *Three Wise Fools*.

The Clark Music Company had to turn down hundreds of orders for the innovative small harp. When Melville Clark died in 1953, his dream for a fiberglass harp had resulted in fewer than thirty experimental models. One can only imagine how popular his "lightweight, inexpensive, indestructible" harp would be today. Clark would have to be pleased at the success of the colorful and popular Rees Harpsicles.[54]

During Clark's lifetime his harps were used in concerts on the great stages of the day: Boston Symphony Hall, Carnegie Hall in New York City, Chicago Symphony Hall, Severance Hall in Cleveland, Armory Hall in Detroit, Erards Hall in Paris, and the White House.[55]

Melville Clark's harps were easily carried and were played around the world, from mountaintops to under the sea. In 1918 Clark played

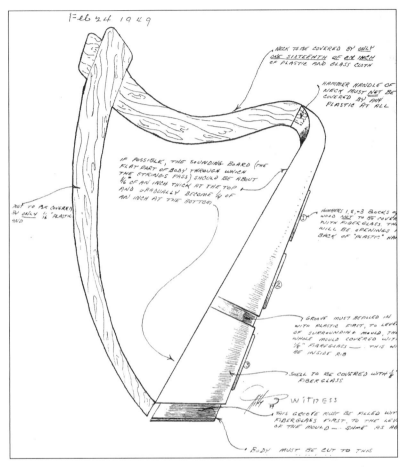

Clark's sketch of the Timothy Clark Plastic (Fiberglass) Harp, February 24, 1949.

on top of Mount Wilson, California, near Pasadena; in 1948 on a plane flying to London; and in 1949 in a submerged submarine off New Haven, Connecticut. Among the Clark papers are invoices for the instrument from six continents. One of the most remote destinations from which an order was received was Cameroon, Africa, in 1926.[56]

One of the longest journeys a Clark Irish Harp ever made was from New York City to Little America, Antarctica. The harp, owned by Clark, was loaned to Dr. F. Dana Coman, medical adviser on Cdr. Richard E. Byrd's first expedition to the South Pole. Dr. Coman was in charge of diet and overall health for the expedition members and ship's crew. A graduate of Syracuse University, he had learned to play the instrument in Syracuse.[57]

In 1928 Byrd refitted and strengthened a Norwegian sealer, the *Samson*, built for sailing into icy waters. Renamed the *City of New York*, it left Hoboken, New Jersey, on August 25, making for Dunedin, New Zealand, via the Panama Canal.[58] The *City of New York*, carrying the Byrd party and a thirty-man crew, sailed into Dunedin after three months at sea. They reloaded the ship with supplies for

Melville Clark playing his harp on Mount Wilson, California, 1918.

fifteen months, so that if the *City of New York* were the only ship to make it through into the Bay of Whales, they would have enough supplies to maintain a limited scientific expedition for at least one year. They took on dogsled teams and additional scientists, and a Fairchild folding-wing monoplane was lashed to the ship's deck.[59]

On December 28, 1928, the *City of New York* reached the Bay of Whales and found a place along the edge of the ice where it could tie up. Commander Byrd and four other men went ashore, found a suitable site for the scientific headquarters eight miles from the ship, and named it Little America. On a good day each dog team made two round-trips, hauling supplies from the ship to their new home. In all, 650 tons of stores and materials were transferred. The *City of New York* had successfully transported one airplane, twelve hundred gallons of gasoline, seventy-five tons of coal, fifty-four men, eighty dogs, enough food for fifteen months, and a Clark Irish Harp.[60]

Melville Clark received a postcard dated and postmarked February 1, 1929, SS *City of New York*, Byrd Antarctic Expedition, stating, "We get lots of enjoyment from the Irish Harp from the fingers of Doc Coman." It was signed "C. E. Rofgren, Secretary to Comdr. Byrd." A postscript in pencil along the outer edge read, "So says the *busy* doctor—also [signed] FD Coman."[61]

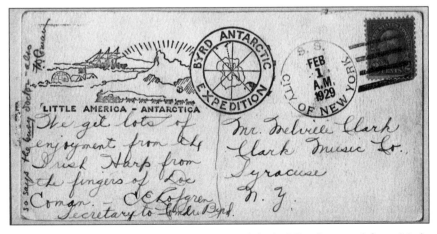

Postcard from C. E. Rofgren, secretary to Admiral Byrd, posted from Little America, Antarctica, February 1, 1929.

Clark received a letter from Dr. Coman and two photos of him playing the harp aboard the ship en route to Antarctica. The letter, dated "Winter Night 1929," reads as follows: "Best wishes from Little America. Can testify that without music we'd all gone cuckoo—and

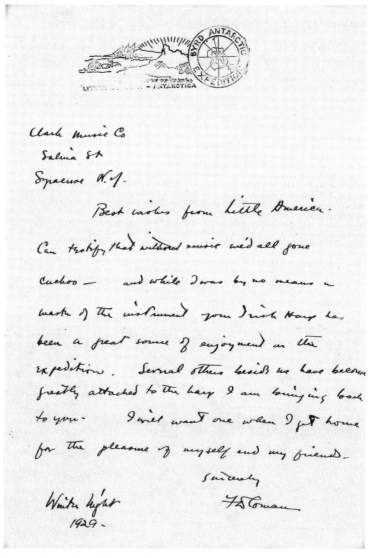

Letter from Dr. F. Dana Coman from Little America, Antarctica, 1929.

while I was by no means a master of the instrument, your Irish Harp has been a great source of enjoyment on this expedition. Several others besides me have become greatly attached to the harp I am bringing back to you. I will want one when I get home for the pleasure of myself and my friends. Sincerely, FD Coman."[62]

The successful Antarctic expedition ended when the men boarded the *City of New York* and left the Bay of Whales on February 6, 1930, sailing back to New Zealand. They arrived there on March 10. After reloading the ship with supplies, the explorers returned to New York City on June 18.[63]

The Clark Music Company received a citation from Rear Adm. Richard E. Byrd and the Executive Committee of the Byrd Aviation Associates expressing their "enduring appreciation of the most valuable co-operation in the equipping of the *Byrd Antarctic Expedition.*" It was signed by "R. E. Byrd, Leader, and James I. Burk, Chairman."[64]

On the deck of the *City of New York,* Dr. Coman holding the Clark Irish Harp, 1928.

Citation from Rear Adm. Richard E. Byrd and the Executive Committee of the Byrd Aviation Associates.

The Clark Irish Harp became the standard against which other folk harps have traditionally been judged. The instrument was in production from 1911 to 1948. Hundreds of them were made in Syracuse and Chicago, and hundreds are still being played today. They are actively sought and proudly displayed. The dream of a young man was fulfilled: to make a beautiful, small, affordable, and transportable harp for all to enjoy.

Additional Details on Harp Construction

The Early Clark Irish Harp

Clark's pre-1911 harp no. 134 is the same height and weight as the standard Clark Irish Harp. It is 39 inches high and weighs 12 pounds. This instrument has a detachable pedestal, or stand. The harp without its pedestal can stand on the floor and easily be played by a child. Both the harp and the pedestal are painted dark green, with decorative shamrocks and other Celtic designs. "Clark Music Co." is stenciled in gilt lettering on the lateral aspect near the top left side of the harp's curvilinear pillar and on one side of the stand. The harp has similar Celtic designs in gilt on the anterior and lateral, top and bottom, aspects of the pillar. The soundboard is painted white, with green shamrock decals cascading from top to bottom, ending with small clusters on each side. The stand is 21 inches high and measures 13½ x 14 inches. A round hole in the center of the stand accommodates a 3-inch bolt, which fastens the harp to the stand with a large wing nut. On the top surface of the stand are four crescent-shaped medallions in a Celtic design, one on each corner. The vertical sides of the stand are decorated with additional Celtic patterns, each about 9 inches long.

There is no knee cap, and the upper head block is large, which Clark believed was tone binding. The thirty-one string holes have no remaining eyelets or crescents to protect the strings from the wood, but one mother-of-pearl peg remains. The four feet of the harp are plain and functional, elliptical in shape, and painted green to match the harp.

On this early Clark harp, the sharping blades, or "fingers," are of three lengths, graduated from 1 to 1½ inches long. They are devoid of note identification and are all without color coding. The blades can be rotated one-quarter turn to rest on the upper part of the string, creating a pitch change one-half step sharper. This simple, original mechanism lacked a spring built into it to maintain the sharped position; it depended on the pressure of the string against the blade. (See fig. 19 with Clark and one of his early models.)

The Standard Clark Irish Harp, 1911–48

Like the early model, the standard Clark Irish Harp is 39 inches high and weighs 12 pounds. The soundboard is 10½ inches wide at the bottom, 3½ inches wide at the top, and 35 inches long. The pillar width is 1⅜ inches. The sides of the body, or shell, are of rock maple with beautiful veneers of bird's-eye or curly maple. The shell contains four rectangular vertical holes, which are placed end-to-end for enhancing the tone quality and supplying a convenient means of handling the instrument. The sounding board is made of spruce or Galician pine, reinforced along its entire length with two strips of bass wood.[65] One strip is applied inside, and the other outside. The strips have holes punched through them to accommodate the thirty-one strings that pass through. Each of the holes, with the exception of the lowest eight, is protected by a pearl-like celluloid insert, which prevents the strings from cutting into the soundboard. The lowest eight strings are wound and have no bridge pins. They are fastened by washers, which allows them to vibrate along their entire length.

Because Clark wanted his harp to be totally portable, he abandoned the early design for the pedestal that the harp sat upon and to which it was attached by a large bolt and wing nut. Instead, in 1911 he designed an adjustable folding base, which would harmonize with the lines of the harp. This base, or taborette, is made of rock maple and stands 13 inches high. The taborettes are numbered identically to the A-model harps because they were sold together as one unit.

Attaching the harp to the taborette is very easy for the player. At its base, made of chestnut, the harp is fitted with two pins that slide into two slots on top of the taborette. Two levers on the taborette turn inward to lock the harp firmly into place. A spring holds the harp in a stable upright position when it is not in use. A single lever at the back of the taborette releases the spring, allowing the instrument to swing back and rest lightly on the player's shoulder. All four feet of the taborette rest squarely on the floor and hold the harp firmly in position, no matter how vigorous the playing.

The harp can easily be detached from the taborette by turning the two side levers outward, releasing the feet of the harp from the base. The taborette itself has collapsible legs, which fold flat for portability, and a locking device for securing the legs. Clark also designed a shoulder strap to support the harp if a harper wished to stand or stroll around playing the instrument.

Clark's list of thirty improvements on the A model included a knee cap, finished in brass, a return spring on the sharping fingers that set into brass sockets, the letter of each string stamped on the corresponding sharping finger, side soundboard strips, upper head block trimmed to allow free vibration of sound, enlarged holes in the bass area of the body to improve tone, colored F and C tuning pins, a shellacked soundboard, a collapsible base, and a khaki waterproof case with upright handle.[66]

TABLE 1. Clark Irish Harp and taborette patents

Date	Purpose	Patent No.
10/10/1911	Adjustable bridge pins, fret for changing pitch of a string	1,005,157
12/5/1911	Base and string-frame tilt ability	1,010,477
12/19/1911	Design for harp as a whole	41,987
3/25/1913	Design of soundboard	639,443
6/24/1913	Folding legs on taborette	1,065,661
8/4/1914	Stamped sharpening fingers	1,105,879
3/30/1915	Shoulder strap to support harp while playing in strolling or standing position	1,133,615
3/30/1915	Colored tuning pins	1,133,616
3/30/1915	Metal strip in back of soundboard	122,519
3/31/1920	Harp improvement, octave fretting	1,351,468
2/19/1922	Harp improvement, double-action octave fretting	1,406,347

Clark Papers, Patent folder, LPK-C

4

Birth of the Nylon Harp String

WHEN MELVILLE CLARK drew his fingers across the strings of his concert harp on February 12, 1948, at a recital in the Syracuse Museum of Fine Arts, he was making musical history. He had realized the ambition of a lifetime, the dream of his father, and the hopes of hundreds of musicians by inventing nylon harp strings.[1] Clark called it "the most thrilling, most heartening musical development in my forty years in the music business."[2]

Before World War I the only harp strings available in the United States were imported from Italy, France, and Germany. In his biography of Carlos Salzedo, *From Aeolian to Thunder,* Dewey Owens states, "The most desirable were the German strings but WWI eliminated that source. American harp dealers tried encouraging local packinghouses to manufacture that all-important commodity. Armour Packing Company of Chicago did produce a usable string; it was orange colored and the C's were dyed green and the F's were dyed purple." The Armour gut string still presented the same centuries-old problems, though: poor durability, uneven tonal quality, and susceptibility to climatic changes.[3]

J. George Morley, a harp maker in London, wrote the following in his 1918 pamphlet, *Hints for the Guidance of the Amateur Harpist:*

> Trouble to harpists, as well as fiddlers, is the imperfection of the gut string, want of truth. Not one string in five hundred is really true; all gut strings are false, more or less. Every gut string fails to give one certain distinct note only. A false string is thicker in one part than another; this produces falsity of intonation. Some gut strings are not round, they are oval; this too produces falsity of intonation.

Musical History Recorded as Clark Plays Harp With New Nylon Strings

Clark playing a concert harp strung with nylon strings for a world premiere, Syracuse Museum of Fine Arts, February 12, 1948. Courtesy of the *Syracuse Post-Standard.*

I have seen a string which in one part of its length stops at third A on the gauge, and in another part of its length goes up to second A, a whole octave difference in the same string. Such a string has its use, to tie up parcels with, but it is of no use on a harp. Tuning is impossible; throw it away.[4]

In 1930 Wallace Hume Carothers, a brilliant scientist at the E. I. du Pont de Nemours Company (du Pont), one day was stirring a molten mass of plastic materials in a vat. When he withdrew the ladle, he noticed long threads clinging to it. The threads could be stretched to four times their original length, reducing the diameter as they lengthened and thinned. This observation was the birth of polymerization, a process made known to the public when nylon was first introduced in 1938.[5]

Shortly after the public announcement of the new microfilament, Clark began consulting with du Pont executives and scientists to persuade them to make nylon strings for harps.[6] He secured a sample of the new fiber from the du Pont labs, but indeed found that the first strands stretched to several times their original length, reducing the diameter by about 50 percent. Clark wrote the company requesting that the filaments be prestretched to make them more stable. He reported, "The Company gladly complied with my wishes."[7]

Scientists at the du Pont laboratories eventually produced the nylon strings Clark specified by extruding nylon through a die to a predetermined thickness. After extrusion, the strings were unwound from a slow-moving spool onto a faster-moving spool, drawing them out 25 percent more. The strings were then shipped to the Clark Music Company in Syracuse, where they were cut to length and placed under steady tension for ten days. The stress on each string was relative to the tension the string would be subjected to on a tuned harp. Then the strings were strung on harps, stretched manually, and tuned a little above pitch, or at greater than normal tension. They were retuned and restretched each day for ten more days in a "settling" process, which made it possible for the strings to hold their final pitch for long periods. The nylon strings had a uniform cross-section and would not fray or become rough even during constant use. Because their tensile strength was seven times greater than the strength of gut strings, the danger of string breakage was substantially decreased.[8]

But Clark needed more than just a nylon string; he required several different gauges of the new product. He requested that du Pont produce twelve different gauges of nylon, ranging from .016" to .060". These strands were strung on four-octave lever harps at the Syracuse harp factory. By 1947 du Pont was capable of producing thirty-two different diameters of strings to Clark's specifications, which allowed a lever harp, as well as a concert or pedal harp, to be strung with a full set of nylon strings for four octaves, including colored strings for the C's and F's.[9] (By 1946 du Pont had perfected the dye formulas for nylon tennis-racket strings in yellow, orange, red, blue, and green. The same technology transferred easily to the manufacture of colored harp strings.)

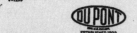

V-1259

E. I. DU PONT DE NEMOURS & COMPANY
INCORPORATED

626 SCHUYLER AVE., ARLINGTON, N. J.

PLASTICS DEPARTMENT   October 16, 1947

Clark Music Company
416 S. Salina St.
Syracuse, N. Y.

ATTENTION: MELVILLE CLARK, PRESIDENT

Dear Mr. Clark:

                    NYLON FILAMENTS

          Thanks very much for your letter of October 3. I am very sorry that I
missed you when you were in New York, but unfortunately, I was away the entire
week of October 6, and was unable to locate you on October 13.

          I am delighted to learn that you are ready to begin to use nylon on the
Clark Irish Harp, and note that you would like us to send you 5 pounds of each of
the diameters which we can produce at the present time. I am listing below the
diameter, the price, and the feet per pound of each size which we can commercially
supply, and I wish that you would look these over since I feel that you may want
to cut down the pounds ordered on certain sizes in view of the fact that the finer
sizes will give you a great deal more feet per pound than the heavier diameters.

OVERSTRUNG-F.G. .016"	$ 9.00 per pound	10,000 feet per pound	LENGTH- 1ST - 1ST OCT	
4T-F .020"	11.00 per pound	6,400 feet per pound	" 1ST - 2nd "	
4T-D- .021"	11.00 per pound	5,800 feet per pound	" 2.5 - 3rd "	
4T-C- .022"	11.00 per pound	5,300 feet per pound	" 4½ - 4T	
4T-B-A-B .023"	11.00 per pound	4,850 feet per pound		
2nd-D-B-4T-F .028"	12.00 per pound	3,250 feet per pound		
2nd-B-C .032"	13.00 per pound	2,500 feet per pound		
2nd-E-B-A .036"	13.00 per pound	1,950 feet per pound		
3d-D-E .040"	13.50 per pound	1,600 feet per pound		
3d-LABL .045"	14.00 per pound	1,250 feet per pound		
4T D-E .055"	14.00 per pound	850 feet per pound		
4T-C .060"	14.00 per pound	600 feet per pound		

          All the above sizes can be supplied to you either in 44" hanks or in
continuous lengths on spools. I would suggest the continuous lengths on spools,
or in coils, since this will cut down the wastage in cutting your strings to the
exact length which you desire.

                              Yours very truly,

                              R. H. Carter

                              R. H. CARTER, NYLON SALES

BETTER THINGS *for* BETTER LIVING...THROUGH CHEMISTRY

"Lucite" acrylic resin • "Plexiglas" cellulose acetate plastic • "Tyglon" cellulose nitrate plastic • "Nylon"
"Pyralin" plastic had on spool • "Polectron" acrylic resin molding material • "Vinylite" polyvinyl resin

String-gauge list from R. H. Carter, du Pont, to Clark, October 16, 1947.
Clark's handwritten calibrations appear in the margins.

Melville A. Clark with four harps strung with nylon strings, 1948.

E. I. du Pont could not produce a nylon filament in sizes heavier than .055". Clark needed .065", .075", and .085" for the lower strings of the fifth octave. But by 1951 du Pont could spin a microfilament of .060", which is a fourth-octave B. A communiqué regarding string issues from the du Pont labs explained, "At this time, we neither have nor know of any process whereby we can spin monofilaments in excess of this diameter, although we are currently attempting to produce .075".".[10] Clark spent eight years testing different gauges of the nylon filaments, but fifth-octave nylon strings were not produced during his lifetime.[11]

Besides frequent string breakage, one of the greatest worries of stringed instrument players is the effect of atmospheric conditions. Nylon is not affected by dampness or humidity because it is not absorbent and dries quickly. Clark found this point to be true when in January 1947 he made a cross-country train trip to Los Angeles to attend a board of directors meeting of the National Association of Music Merchants. He took with him a small harp strung with half gut and half nylon. When he reached the West Coast, three gut strings had broken, but the nylon strings were intact and in tune. Clark exclaimed, "This was proof that I had something. Now I want to tell the world about it. Especially the ten thousand or more harpists of this country."[12]

Three weeks before his recital at the Syracuse Museum of Fine Arts, he contacted the media, announcing the revolutionary new musical string. The *New York Times* wrote, "Nylon, adorner of feminine limbs, is challenging the centuries-old monopoly of sheep gut in the realm of music. It became known yesterday that Melville Clark, harp maker, of Syracuse, New York, has developed a full line of thirty-three gauges of nylon harp strings."[13] Other articles appeared in the musical trade magazines of the late 1940s: *Modern Plastics, Music Trades, Musical Merchandise,* and *Piano Trades.* Clark was proudest of a full-page story in color in *Life* in 1948. It pictured a harpist holding a fiberglass harp strung with nylon strings immersed in a five-foot tank of water (see chapter 3, fig. 22).[14]

The day after his recital, when interviewed by the *Syracuse Post-Standard,* Clark said, "Nylon strings give a clear, brilliant singing tone. The clarity can now be achieved in the upper harp octaves, which heretofore was not obtainable. Aside from the amazing difference in tone, there is the advantage of the playing facility attained by the smoother, slicker nylon strings in addition to the important factor of sturdiness which nylon has over gut. Think what this will mean to

Clark demonstrates that nylon strings are impervious to water, 1948.

the harpist, who has always faced the risk of having a string 'pop' during a concert."[15]

By June 1, 1948, the Clark Music Company had begun packaging four octaves of nylon strings and selling them to harpists all over the world. Because of their durability and their cost, which was 25 percent less than the cost of gut strings, the new strings sold themselves.[16]

Cellists and other string instrumentalists inquired about the availability of nylon strings. In 1948 in an interview for the *New York*

Clark Nylon Harp String packet, First Octave "A."

Times, Clark remarked that "musicians who draw their bows across violins, violas, cellos, and contrabasses cannot use the new strings being produced. Nylon strings are too slippery and whistle under a bow. However, the manufacturers promise a superior nylon 'horse hair' that will make the bows more durable. Mr. Clark predicts that nylon will start a 'great vogue' in the harp." The *Times* columnist went on to write, "Makers of harps hope, of course, that this instrument will become as popular in this world as the next."[17]

Melville A. Clark made a lasting contribution to the musical world. Several companies now package nylon strings with their own label, but the major manufacturer of nylon strings is still the E. I. du Pont Company. Today, more than fifty years after Clark introduced them to the harp world, nylon strings are sold for harps, guitars, ukuleles, balalaikas, and thousands of toy instruments.

5

Inventions and Ideas

MELVILLE A. CLARK will go down in history as the designer and builder of the Clark Irish Harp. That single accomplishment might have been enough for most men, but Clark was energetic and ambitious. He spent his entire lifetime inventing a wide variety of new devices and designing improvements for existing ones. He even had special writing paper imprinted with the heading "Ideas" on which to set his schemes.

Clark's greatest successes came with the design and improvements of the Clark Irish Harp, nylon strings for musical instruments, the mechanical Clark "No Bruise" Fruit Picker, and an automatic record changer. Other inventions, such as a marine escape, an auto guard, and a tone amplifier, remained at the development stage and never got into production during his lifetime.

Fruit Picker

The Clark Fruit Picker was one of Melville Clark's earliest inventions. While traveling through the orchard country near Sandusky, Ohio, in 1902, Melville Clark saw hundreds of peach trees. Women were doing most of the harvesting. He noticed they were not using ladders but standing on the ground, reaching up to pick the fruit with their hands, a slow and tedious process. The peaches were difficult to reach and awkward to pick without pulling out the stems. When picking fruit by hand, one is apt to inadvertently destroy the tiny buds that represent the next season's fruit crop. These observations inspired Clark to work on developing a tool for harvesting the fruit more efficiently.[1]

Over the next eight years, Clark worked on several models of mechanical fruit pickers, all of which he eventually abandoned. The

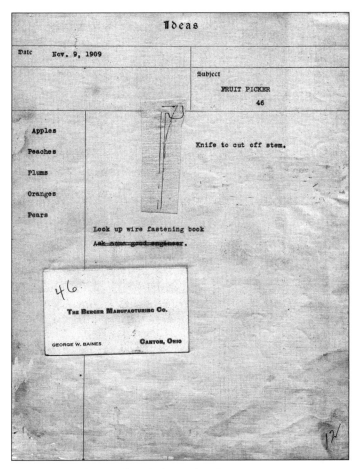

Letterhead of Melville Clark's "Ideas" stationery.

experimenting cost him several hundred dollars, and success seemed far away. Finally, in 1911, Clark conceived yet another idea for the device. He took his sketches to Spencer Eggleston, a mechanical engineer in Syracuse. Eggleston drew up a design for patenting and producing the fruit picker, according to Clark's specifications.[2]

Clark's "tool" was simple to operate and inexpensive to make. It consisted of a small wire basket shaped like a crown. Open at the top and bottom, it was connected at the lower end to a canvas tube and was mounted on a five-foot or longer bamboo pole. The person gathering the fruit could stand on the ground and reach up into tree branches with the pole. A row of triangular wire teeth, slightly converging and with sharp lateral edges, encircled the upper rim of the cage. The blades of adjoining teeth formed a series of "reciprocal knives" that would nip off the fruit at the stem by a pull or twist of the pole. The fruit fell neatly into the cage and slid smoothly through the canvas tube into a

Patent for Clark "No Bruise" Fruit Picker invention, October 1, 1929.

basket swung from the operator's shoulder. The bag could hold one to two quarts of fruit. Clark designed the new tool in three sizes, suitable for picking apples, peaches, plums, lemons, oranges, apricots, cherries, and nuts. He called it the "Clark 'No Bruise' Fruit Picker."[3]

The Fruit Picker was lightweight, making it easy to lift into the highest reaches of a tree. To a great extent it obviated the need for a ladder, but by using a short bamboo handle, the tool could be used in conjunction with one. It was well adapted to picking fruit not only in large orchards but also in home gardens and small orchards, which were commonplace in the early part of the twentieth century.

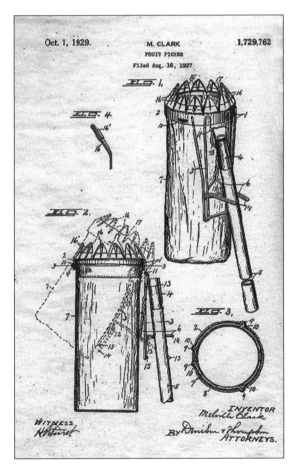

Patent drawing of the Clark Fruit Picker, October 1, 1929.

Clark received a patent for his Fruit Picker in 1912. He continued to tinker with the design and received another patent for an improved version in 1929.[4]

The metal parts were manufactured in Worcester, Massachusetts, by the C. E. Kilbourne Company. The firm was the household specialty division of the National Manufacturing Company of that city.[5] The finished metallic parts of the pickers were then shipped to the Federal Flag Corporation in Cortland, New York, to make and attach the cotton catch-bags. The firm had a reputation for using high-quality cotton for making flags. Although no stars and stripes were considered for the fabric's design, Clark did specify that the bags should be orange in color and should be able to withstand frequent washings.[6]

The Fruit Pickers sold for $1.50 each, and Clark himself did a lot of the marketing. Curiously, the advertising copy for the Clark Fruit Picker was written on the Clark Music Company letterhead.

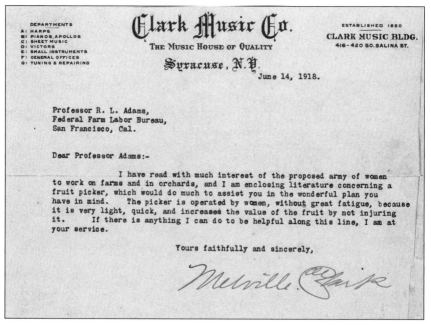

Clark Music Co. letterhead used to promote sales of the Clark Fruit Picker.

Record Changer

Clark's record-changing device was another successful and profitable invention. Clark and Paul Wilbur, an engineer from Syracuse, produced it jointly. It was a combination of a turntable, a record stack with a magazine or carrying member, and a mechanical means for moving one of the records out of the stack to the magazine. The device facilitated the playing of records on both sides without human assistance. The two men received a patent for their invention in 1928. They sold the patent in 1932 to Capehart Automatic Phonograph Company of Fort Wayne, Indiana, for $5,000. This device was incorporated into thousands of jukeboxes that Capehart manufactured, for which Clark and Wilbur received royalties.[7]

Marine Escape

Bearing in mind sea disasters such as the sinking of the *Titanic* in 1912 and the burning of the *Morro Castle* offshore near Asbury Park, New Jersey, in 1934, Clark and his attorney, Virgil H. Clymer, became involved in designing a system for marine escape.[8] An unlikely pair, Clark the music man and Clymer the lawyer modified and perfected an existing fire-escape device to use on passenger ships.[9] The device had a looplike belt that a passenger could slip around his or her body, under the arms, after donning an inflated rubber jacket. The belt was attached to a cable, which was impervious to fire or saltwater. The slightest weight caused the cable to automatically uncoil at a fixed speed from a metal box clamped to the stateroom wall. A passenger could escape out his porthole, being gently lowered toward the water.

Several steamship lines embraced the new invention. However, authorization for installation of any sort on a passenger ship needed to come from the Department of Commerce. It seems that the portholes, or air ports, were being downsized, making them too small for a person to escape through. A letter to Clark from the secretary of the Senate Technical Committee explained, "The air ports are kept small because of the difficulty in keeping them tight. The smaller they are, the stronger they can be made and the tighter they can be kept."[10]

Thus, the pair's well-intentioned device was never marketed. But, not to be dismayed, the two commenced work on an improved lifesaving vest with an extended bobber to expedite rescue at sea.[11]

Auto Guard

By 1925 U.S. urban populations were getting around more with automobiles than with horses. Concerned about the alarming number of collisions, Clark set out to design a metal guard to minimize the damages. He had perfected one by 1927, calling it the "Auto Guard." A blueprint of the design was sent to the National Underwriters conference in New York City with this message: "Auto Guard makes it impossible for cars to do anything but slide by each other. Ten points of contacts are removed where cars would be locked on or bumped. Auto Guard will simply skid them off."[12]

The safety device encircled an auto below the chassis at midwheel level. Clark said of it, "It has a springlike quality that in coming in contact with any rigid member, helps to ease off a direct bump. The front and rear bumpers are so arranged that a direct head-on collision could not take place, but would be thwarted off to one side."[13]

Clark tried to sell his Auto Guard idea to many different American auto manufacturers, but each company replied that it already had its own in-house design and development staff. In 1936 he wrote to Karl Kettering, an executive at General Motors, "Don't you think the time has come when automobiles should have a guard completely surrounding the car? It would also lend length to the shorter cars' appearance and a new idea for 1937 pocketbooks."[14]

Clark continued trying to catch the attention of auto manufacturers for another fifteen years, seeking to persuade them to incorporate his Auto Guard into their designs. In 1950 he wrote to Henry Ford III, of the Ford Motor Company in Detroit, Michigan, and Carl J. Barbie, in the Patent Department of Nash Motors in Kenosha, Wisconsin. Both replied politely that their companies were not interested in his design.[15]

Clark was granted patent-pending status on his Auto Guard.[16] No documentation has been found in his personal papers, however, to

verify that he obtained a patent on the device or that the ‹
ever adopted by an auto manufacturer.

Melville Clark's passionate interest in the burgeoning auto industry was ironic in that he spent as little time as possible behind the
wheel. According to his son Melville Jr., his father had a young driver
(the collections officer for the company), Ernest Groves, who drove
him to work every morning and back home every night. He made his
home with the Clarks for many years. After Groves left the area, Mrs.
Clark did most of the driving for the couple.

Tone Amplifier

Having played the harp for thirty years, Melville Clark was well aware
of its acoustic limitations, especially in an orchestral setting. He
invented a device to amplify instrumental tones and maintain the true
sound of the instrument being played. In 1933 he received a patent
for the amplifier.[17]

Clark described his invention this way: "The device functions by
means of a pin inserted in the sounding board of a stringed instrument, in exactly the place where the sound is best reflected. From this
pin, the intimate vibrations of the instrument are carried through
electrical amplifiers to a pickup, similar to those used on modern
phonographs, a foot pedal control and a portable amplifier." Else-
where, he said, "The player can regulate the volume of his instrument, controlled through a rheostat and amplified by radio tubes.
But there is also a resistance (rheostat mechanism) placed on the
podium, giving the conductor actual control of the entire string section of his orchestra."[18]

Leopold Stokowski, conductor and musical director of the Philadelphia Orchestra, tested Clark's invention on the contrabass. He was
quite enthused with the results and sent a telegram to the *Syracuse
Journal* on January 14, 1932, as follows: "Melville Clark's device will
amplify the tone of any orchestral instrument with flexibility so that
any desired frequencies can be increased in intensity in any ratio with
other frequencies possible on instrument in question. Impossible now
to foresee complete potentiality that may be developed."

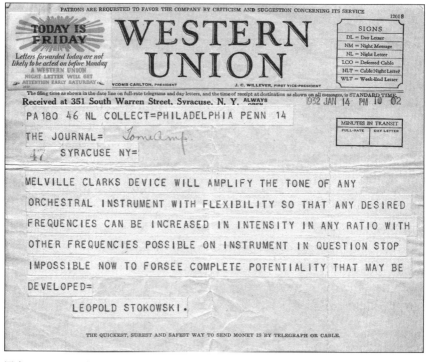

PATRONS ARE REQUESTED TO FAVOR THE COMPANY BY CRITICISM AND SUGGESTION CONCERNING ITS SERVICE

12018

TODAY IS FRIDAY

Letters forwarded today are not likely to be acted on before Monday A WESTERN UNION NIGHT LETTER WILL GET ATTENTION EARLY SATURDAY

WESTERN UNION

VCOMB CARLTON, PRESIDENT   J. C. WILLEVER, FIRST VICE-PRESIDENT

SIGNS
DL = Day Letter
NM = Night Message
NL = Night Letter
LCO = Deferred Cable
NLT = Cable Night Letter
WLT = Week-End Letter

The filing time as shown in the date line on full-rate telegrams and day letters, and the time of receipt at destination as shown on all messages, is STANDARD TIME.

Received at 351 South Warren Street, Syracuse, N. Y. ALWAYS OPEN   1932 JAN 14 PM 10 02

PA180 46 NL COLLECT=PHILADELPHIA PENN 14

MINUTES IN TRANSIT
FULL-RATE   DAY LETTER

THE JOURNAL= *Tone Amp.*

47 SYRACUSE NY=

MELVILLE CLARKS DEVICE WILL AMPLIFY THE TONE OF ANY ORCHESTRAL INSTRUMENT WITH FLEXIBILITY SO THAT ANY DESIRED FREQUENCIES CAN BE INCREASED IN INTENSITY IN ANY RATIO WITH OTHER FREQUENCIES POSSIBLE ON INSTRUMENT IN QUESTION STOP IMPOSSIBLE NOW TO FORSEE COMPLETE POTENTIALITY THAT MAY BE DEVELOPED=

LEOPOLD STOKOWSKI.

THE QUICKEST, SUREST AND SAFEST WAY TO SEND MONEY IS BY TELEGRAPH OR CABLE.

Telegram to Clark from Leopold Stokowski, conductor of the Philadelphia Symphony, January 14, 1932.

The *New York Evening Post* on January 14, 1932, stated: "The adoption of Clark's invention came after two exhaustive tests by Leopold Stokowski during which it was applied to several instruments, notably the double bass, cello and harp. Mr. Stokowski plans to increase the diapason of his orchestra by using banks of the Clark amplifiers on the string section."

After the success in Philadelphia, several other newspapers reported on Clark's invention. The *Christian Science Monitor* headline read, "He Makes It Roar Like Niagara." The *Syracuse Journal* proclaimed on page 1, "Syracusan's Device Opens New Music Era."[19]

Clark's invention was an early example of a means for increasing the volume of a musical instrument by electricity. Clark called

Melville Clark with tone amplifier, *Syracuse Herald-Journal,*
January 14, 1932.

it "enlarging upon the acoustic perfection of instruments already
developed."[20]

Clark had limited success with his tone-amplifier invention. The
fast-expanding field of electric amplification became crowded with
American as well as European devices and improvements. There are
no data to support the idea of an entire symphony string section
amplifying its individual instruments. Shortly after Clark's invention,
improved systems for amplifying entire orchestras were developed.

Ideas, Patents, and Further Inventions

Several of Clark's 1930s ideas and inventions probably came about because the Clark family sold "white goods," stoves and refrigerators, next door to their music store during the Depression in the 1930s.[21] Clark's papers document his design for an "on" and "off" automatic switch for defrosting refrigerators (1930) and a temperature control on refrigerator compartments (1938).[22]

In 1936 Clark's Bon-Air Silent Motor (BASM) was designed and patented. It was a motor built for buses and Pullman cars, to move air into the coach. Clark described its usefulness: "When it is very cold or rainy outside, it is difficult to get ventilation inside. Without water coming in and where the passengers want no draft, the answer is the BASM."[23]

Visualite was a finish Clark developed in 1947 for preventing wooden musical instruments from cracking and drying out. The Visualite formula was kept secret, and Clark used it to coat the harps and other musical instruments in his store inventory, including drumheads. He applied it to both sides of the harp soundboards and inside and outside clarinets and oboes. Visualite was described as being effective for stain proofing, waterproofing, and expediting cleaning; it could resist high temperatures.[24]

On his special "Ideas" stationery, Clark sketched plans for a wide variety of inventions and renovations: a stumbling protector for roller skates, nonskid bars of soap, an automatic news camera, portable phone booths, bicycle safety features, and moving sidewalks.

Clark was very interested in making improvements in the auto industry. His papers contain copies of letters sent to Detroit auto manufacturers and *Popular Science* in which he proposed "wired" glass to prevent icing and fogging, bulletproof glass (1931), a free-wheeling hydraulic clutch, a nonexpanding piston (1935), an oil-pack clutch (1931), and road sanders for cars (1938). Clark wrote: "The road sander is a simple and inexpensive device that consists of two sandboxes on either side of the rear of the car and a pedal that works with the application of the brake and deposits sand in front of the rear wheels, bringing the car to a safe stop in slippery weather."[25] Apparently, he was on the right track, as designers in the auto industry recognized similar problems that Clark had identified. With their access to research labs, equipment, and materials, some of the very designs Clark had sketched on his "Ideas" stationery were the same improvements seen in the cars rolling off the assembly lines in Detroit.

Many of his ideas in the 1940s were a consequence of World War II. An article printed in the September 15, 1945, issue of the *Christian Science Monitor* titled "Let the Lady Speak" describes Clark's scheme to "voice" the Statue of Liberty for welcoming home troopships as they pulled into New York Harbor.

Other ideas that he partially developed from 1943 to 1945 for the war effort included protective, lightweight soft armor, an airplane wing deicer, and a waterproof suit with a breathing helmet to don in case a ship was sinking.[26]

The developer of the Clark Irish Harp had far-reaching ideas and visions that touched people beyond the world of the harp.

Uncle Melville Clark, 1911, Chicago.

P T M
Piano Trade Magazine

AUGUST, 1942

15c A COPY
$1.50 A YEAR

Vol. 39   No. 8

THE JOURNAL OF MUSICAL INSTRUMENT RETAILING

EDITED BY ROY E. WAITE   •   20 EAST JACKSON BOULEVARD, CHICAGO

Photo by Underwood & Underwood, Washington, D. C.

MELVILLE CLARK
Merchant-Division President National Association of Music Merchants

Melville Clark, president of the National Association of Music Merchants, on the cover of *Piano Trade Magazine,* August 1942.

Elaine Vito, NBC harpist, playing the Clark fiberglass harp underwater, *Life*, December 13, 1948. Photo by George Karger of Pix, courtesy of Life, Inc.

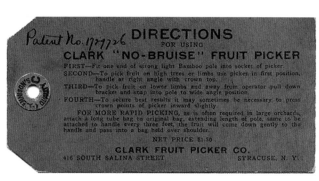

Sales tag for the Clark Fruit Picker.

TEMPLE THEATRE

SEVENTH
SYMPHONY CONCERT
(Subscription Series)

ASSISTING ARTIST
SERGE
PROKOFIEFF
Distinguished Composer Pianist

SYRACUSE SYMPHONY ORCHESRTRA
Conductor, VLADIMIR SHAVITCH

PROKOFIEFF

Conductor
VLADIMIR SHAVITCH

Sat., Feb. 27
at Noon

Tickets Now On Sale,
Prices: 50c, 75c, $1.00, $1.25
At Clark Music Store and Symphony
Office, 212 Cahill Bldg.

Mr. Prokofieff, who was soloist with the Boston Symphony
last night in Carnegie Hall, played his own third piano concerto which is a very brilliantly written work full of rhythmical
energy and interest, scintillant, youthful, audacious in its manner. Mr. Prokofieff enjoyed a triumph with the virtuoso piece
which he had provided himself, He played a very difficult and
effective piano part most brilliantly and was monarch of all he surveyed.
---Olin Downes in the New York Times, Feb. 6, 1926

Playbill for Prokofieff's concert, February 27, 1926.

Cover of souvenir program from the Song and Light Festival, August 9, 1917.

IRELAND

NEW SOUTH WALES

ITALY

ESTONIA   RUSSIA   MONSTERRAT

Stamps from Ireland, New South Wales (Australia), Italy, Estonia, Russia, and Montserrat.

THE SCHIRMER-CLARK COLLECTION

of

RARE MUSIC BOXES

G. SCHIRMER, INC.
NEW YORK

Cover of the catalog of the Schirmer-Clark Collection of Rare Music Boxes.

6

The First Syracuse
Symphony Orchestra

THE CITY OF SYRACUSE, NEW YORK, experienced a cultural renaissance in the thirty years that followed the 1893 Chicago World's Fair. It was a good time and a good place for the Clark Music Company to be in business. In 1901 the Syracuse University Chorus, under the direction of Dr. Howard Lyman, developed into a weeklong music festival that took place in July. The festival chorus included about five hundred of the best voices in the area. Soloists from the world's leading operatic organizations were invited to participate, and the nation's leading orchestras fulfilled the instrumental requirements of the festival. Most popular were Nikolai Sokoloff's Cleveland Orchestra and the Chicago Symphony under the baton of Frederick Stock.

Several times throughout this period, local instrumental musicians would gather in numbers great enough to constitute a symphony orchestra. These professional musicians attracted such large crowds of Syracusans that a group of artistically minded citizens began to think about the possibility of forming a proper symphony with a season subscription. The following is an account of how the first Syracuse Symphony got started, rose to great heights, and then slowly lost its impetus during the Great Depression and World War II.

Eleven symphony orchestras had been established in the United States by 1921. Symphonies in Boston, Cleveland, Philadelphia, Chicago, St. Louis, and New York were among the leaders. Neighboring cities had their patrons. Rochester had George Eastman, and Buffalo, whose Philharmonic was not founded until 1934, received a million dollars in 1935 from George and Mary Kleinhans, for the construction of a music hall. Without fanfare and without one cent, the small city of Syracuse launched a symphony of sixty-one "players."[1]

One of the driving forces behind this organization was Melville Clark, president of the Clark Music Company. The first chartered Syracuse Symphony Orchestra (SSO) began in a modest way in July 1921, when Clark engaged a man named Henri De Pavaloff to organize a symphony and begin rehearsals. De Pavaloff, manager for Alfred Mirovitch, a concert pianist, was then a visiting violinist at the Syracuse University School of Music.[2]

Many of the musicians selected for the symphony were theater orchestral employees who performed with traveling vaudeville acts and also played for the silent movies at the local Strand, Empire, B. F. Keith, Crescent, Temple, and Savoy theaters. Other musicians were businessmen in the community who performed music as an avocation. One exception was a much needed bassoonist, who commuted from Mohawk, New York, an hour away.[3]

Rehearsals began in August 1921 with fifty musicians, who gathered in the Clark Music Building in downtown Syracuse. For a short time rehearsals were held in the old Grand Opera House, later returning to the Clark building.[4] After De Pavaloff had led the group through eleven rehearsals, he was released from his position because of conflicts in his personal and professional schedules. A committee composed of musicians appointed by the principal in each section of the orchestra voted to engage Dr. William Berwald as conductor and music director of the Syracuse University Orchestra.[5] Myron Levee was appointed concertmaster.[6]

The first rehearsal under Dr. Berwald was held at the new B. F. Keith Theatre, adjacent to the Clark Music Company, on December 12, 1921.[7] To establish this new civic endeavor, Edward F. Albee, president of the B. F. Keith Circuit, generously donated for one year the use of the theater, including ushers, tickets, and staging equipment.[8] Manager W. Dayton Wegeforth, another leading force, stated,

"Keith's interest in the enterprise is entirely philanthropic and all players must have union sanction, registered with the union here." The cooperation of George F. Wilson, secretary of the local musicians union, greatly assisted the new symphony in securing the players.[9]

A board of officers was formed to organize the Syracuse Symphony Orchestra, with Melville Clark as president. There were nine officers and thirty trustees. The president, vice president, first vice president, general manager, business manager, and assistant treasurer made up the first executive committee. The executive offices were maintained on the second floor of the Clark Music Building.[10]

The first concert of the new SSO was planned for noon on Saturday, January 21, 1922, with a final rehearsal the morning before the concert. New music stands, folios, programs, and lunches for the musicians were ready. Tickets went on sale: twenty-five cents for orchestra seating and fifteen cents for balcony seating. There were no reserved

The first Syracuse Symphony Orchestra board officers, 1922. *Seated, left to right:* Rudolph Miller, D. T. Brennan (librarian), Melville Clark (president), George Wilson (secretary), Henry Hambrecht, and Paul Hadley. *Standing:* Myron Levee, Aurin Chase (vice president), and Ralph Palmatier (assistant secretary).

D. T. Brennan, Music Committee member, 1922.

seats for this first concert. After the doors opened at eleven thirty, 3,000 people were seated, 150 stood, and 500 to 700 were turned away.[11] The concert was a huge success.

The musicians were paid with proceeds from ticket sales. In a letter to Victor Herbert, Melville Clark wrote, "The Syracuse Symphony Orchestra is founded on the same basis as the London Symphony, on a cooperative basis." And in a letter to the *Music Trade Indicator*, Clark wrote, "This Symphony was established through the cooperation of the players, who are to receive a pro-rata share of the sum taken in and none of the officers will receive a penny."[12]

The first paycheck each player received was in the amount of ten dollars: two dollars for the rehearsal and eight dollars for the concert, which exceeded original expectations that each musician would receive six dollars. Conductor Berwald received ten dollars for the rehearsal and twenty-five dollars for the concert.[13]

Endorsements were secured from prominent musicians and politicians of the time. Among them were Victor Herbert; pianists Ignaz Paderewski, Percy Grainger, and Harold Bauer; President Warren Harding; former governor of New York Nathan Miller; and Syracuse mayor John H. Walwrath. These endorsements were listed on the SSO stationery and other SSO publicity items, in addition to the names of the executive board and committee members.[14]

In a letter to the Syracuse Chamber of Commerce, Clark wrote, "The Syracuse Symphony's first year successes prevailed over the

Syracuse Symphony Orchestra stationery, 1923–24.

concerns of no money in the treasury to start with, no endowment fund, and no backing of a single wealthy person."[15]

Publicity efforts were well organized from the start. According to the SSO president's report, there were 1,500 pieces of advertising matter, 1,400 inches of news coverage in the local newspapers, 4,300 large advertising cards, 104 stories sent to all newspapers, announcements made in 24 clubs, and 8,371 letters sent out. The story of this orchestra's unique formation was covered in 455 newspapers across the country.[16]

Before the third concert, scheduled for March 23, 1922, a Young People's Concert was offered to children over the age of eight. It preceded the regular concert by one hour and probably served as a dress rehearsal. A letter from Clark to Professor Shea of the Lincoln School lays out an elaborate, almost comical, plan for the children's entrance into the Keith Theatre. Students from twelve local schools were to assemble in front of specific stores. A letter sent to the chaperone or teacher of each school read, "Prof. Shea of Lincoln School will await the gathering of the children at the Keith Theatre entrance to assign them to their section in the theatre. The schools will assemble in front of the various businesses in the 400 block [of South Salina Street] and will be admitted in the order in which they arrive."[17]

In a letter to Anna Morrison, events editor of the *Syracuse Journal,* Clark stated, "To make it interesting for the children, we are to give them a very careful explanation of the theme as played by each instrument. This shows them the color possibilities. Imagine their surprise when they hear the entire battery of the orchestra, which is certainly loud and lusty."[18]

During the first season, January through June 1922, the orchestra played five regular concerts and two Young People's Concerts, with the house crowded for every event. By April the orchestra had grown to seventy-five players. The success of the first season generated great enthusiasm for planning the orchestra's second season.[19] In minutes recorded at the end of the second year, the president thanked the executive committee for attending thirty meetings, from September 1921 to June 1923.[20]

The Syracuse Symphony Orchestra, Dr. William Berwald, conductor, 1922.

Edward Albee once again donated the Keith Theatre for rehearsals and concerts planned for the upcoming season, and he again assumed a portion of the SSO's expenses.[21] The second season offered seven regular concerts and six Young People's Concerts. The goal for the Young People's Concerts was to make it possible for eighteen thousand children to experience a live musical performance.[22]

During the third season, Dr. Berwald announced that he would be unable to continue his work with the SSO in the fall. Pressures of work at Syracuse University had become too great for him to hold both positions. For a time, his resigning seemed to threaten the life of the new orchestra. But shortly after Berwald's notification, a very capable guest conductor was introduced to Syracuse audiences.[23]

The solo artists and guest conductors who appeared with the symphony for the first few years did so on a no-fee basis. The SSO paid for their expenses, which included hotels, meals, and railroad fares.[24] One of these guest artists was Tina Lerner. She was described as a beautiful young Russian pianist who had studied at the Moscow Philharmonic Conservatory from 1896 to 1904. On March 29, 1924, the sixth concert of the third season, she performed Wagner's *Overture to Rienzi*. The guest conductor for the evening was her husband, Vladimir Shavitch, conductor of the Theatre Orchestra in the neighboring

B. F. Keith Theatre's interior, 1920. Collection of the
Onondaga Historical Association.

city of Rochester, New York. The couple received rave reviews,[25] and
Shavitch was soon hired for five thousand dollars as music director
and conductor for the symphony.[26]

   In July 1924, before the beginning of his first season with the
SSO, conductor Shavitch received a letter from the L. G. Sharpe concert agency in London. It read, "I have the pleasure informing you
that at a meeting held last evening, the Directors of the London Symphony agreed to invite you to conduct the fifth Symphony Concert of
the nineteenth series to be held at Queen's Hall, London, on Monday
evening January 12, 1925, and that they would be pleased to extend

Tina Lerner, pianist, 1924.

this invitation to Madame Tina Lerner to play a concerto at this concert."[27] Shavitch was granted a four-week leave of absence to fulfill this engagement abroad. He was the only American guest conductor that year to lead the world-famous London Symphony Orchestra, thus reversing the usual pattern of European leaders coming as guests to the United States.[28]

The Syracuse community was justly proud of this invitation. Local newspapers headlined the honor their new music director and his wife had achieved. It was front-page copy when they received the invitation, when they departed for the trip, and once again when they returned.[29] On all his billing abroad, including posters and handbills, the line under Shavitch's name read, "Conductor of the Syracuse Symphony,

Vladimir Shavitch, conductor, 1924.

USA." Tina Lerner performed Tchaikovsky's Pianoforte Concerto in B-flat Minor at their evening performance.

When the couple returned to upstate New York on February 2, 1925, the *Syracuse Telegram* printed Shavitch's photo with the caption, "Vladimir Shavitch conductor of the Syracuse Symphony is back in Syracuse after having accomplished the dual mission of placing Syracuse on the music map of the world and winning the unequivocal approval of the most conservative musical audience under the sun, the subscription audience of the London Symphony Orchestra."

The SSO's fourth season, 1924–25, was to be a turning point for this young and fast-growing institution. One of the artists who performed in the fourth season under the new conductor was John

McCormack, a world-class tenor. He was accommodated at the newly opened Hotel Syracuse for his November 13 concert.[30]

Victor Herbert of Lake Placid was a great supporter of the new symphony. After his death, in the spring of 1924, Melville Clark wrote the Herbert family inquiring about the disposition of the very large Victor Herbert music library.[31] This music collection included thousands of folios of classical and standard works, in addition to many compositions, arrangements, and writings of this noted musician. When the family had it appraised, it was valued at eight thousand dollars.[32] Mrs. C. E. Crouse (the former Alta Pease, founder of the Salon Musicals and a concert contralto) made a contribution of one thousand dollars toward the purchase. With this nucleus to build on, other members of the Salon Musicals contributed enough to purchase the extensive library. Melville Clark said, "The orchestra has the very best facilities for caring for the valuable addition to its already large collection of musical works. The SSO will now be in a position to go ahead on even more extended lines than before."[33]

With a world-class music director in place, the SSO was taken on as a civic enterprise, becoming chartered in 1925.[34] Melville Clark had founded the fledgling orchestra and had maintained it for four years. After the charter was established and new board members were elected, Clark stepped down from his executive position to be one of the board members. In a synopsis of the history of the SSO from 1921 to 1924, Clark wrote the following:

> A small group of public-spirited citizens has now assumed the guidance of the Syracuse Symphony. I will return to give my attention to my personal affairs. My activities in the management will end with the organization of the new committee, headed by Martin Knapp.[35] This is made obligatory because of the demand of the board of directors of the Clark Music Co. that I give more time to it and less to outside interests. The SSO is now on sound footing, with the players paid for rehearsals and concerts and a great conductor, Mr. Shavitch.[36]

Clark remained an active board member for the next nine years.

In December 1924 Albee reported to the SSO board that Keith's could no longer extend the theater to the orchestra for free, because of its $60,000 business loss that year. Each of the fourteen remaining concerts would cost $250 to be held at Keith's. For the first time the SSO would need sponsors for each concert. Increased expenses for printing, publicity, and music transformed the very successful SSO into a very expensive organization.[37]

An editorial in the *Syracuse Sunday American* on March 2, 1925, suggested a campaign to raise funds for the SSO. It was an appeal to the public for donations: "The people of Syracuse must join without delay in giving the SSO the one conclusive proof of their willingness to support it. Adequate revenue must be secured and now is the time to begin." A deficit of $5,500 was quickly reduced to $3,000 by donations from music patrons, but no formal fund-raising drive was organized at this time.[38]

Support for the SSO came in other forms. It was determined that further planning for the twenty-four-year-old weeklong music festival, held every July, should cease. The minutes of the board meeting of March 11, 1925, read as follows:

> WHEREAS, it is the sentiment of this Board that the Syracuse Symphony Orchestra fills to a large extent the purposes for which the Central New York Music Festival Association was formed and it is this Board's desire to avoid any possibility of competition with the SSO in obtaining popular interest and support, and to aid in the growth and development of the SSO until it is firmly established as a permanent institution in Syracuse.
>
> RESOLVED, that future Music Festivals under this Board be indefinitely postponed.[39]

At the beginning of the SSO's fifth season, the Saturday noon-time regular subscription concerts moved to the Temple Theatre at 424 South Salina Street, and the new popular concerts moved to the Armory on Sunday evenings.[40] A series of Young People's Concerts was held in the Lincoln Auditorium of Central High School. A press release on October 29, 1925, stated, "The Board of Education has granted Mr. Shavitch the following privileges: permission to use the Central H. S. Auditorium and appointed teachers only to be admitted to the concerts."[41]

The first organized fund-raising campaign began when the orchestra's Women's Committee staged a drive to raise $30,000 for the deficit fund. Campaign chairman Evalina Honsinger, president of Morning Musicals, initiated it on January 31, 1926, engaging 150 Syracuse women to participate. Corporate board chairman John Derschung, founder and president of Easy Washer Company, stated the need for this campaign: "The cost of a concert is $3,000. With every seat sold at the Temple Theatre it is worth only $1,500. At the Armory for the popular concerts, at capacity is worth only $1,350. The deficit for the coming season will be between $25,000 and $30,000, even with the most businesslike management. According to figures obtained by the SSO Committee, no similar organization in this Country is being carried on without a deficit of at least $100,000."[42]

With a successful fund-raising campaign under way, the next big project was to find an auditorium more suitable to perform in than the movie theaters. Louis Crabtree, music critic for the local newspaper, addressed the issue:

> We should be enjoying our musical fare in a well-appointed hall, large enough to allow 5,000 of us to sit down comfortable, and not gulping down on Saturday noons in much the same way as we swallow a hasty lunch and rush back to the office without loss of time. And yet, such is the apparent determination of the community to support and enjoy its symphony, that not on a single occasion during the season has the management had cause to complain of lax attendance, but, on the contrary, bumper and overflowing audiences have been the rule.[43]

A permanent home for the SSO was not readily found. The orchestra went from the Temple Theatre back to Keith's in 1926, then on to the Strand Theatre in 1928.[44] The last home for the group was the Lincoln Auditorium in Central High School, where the Young People's Concerts had been presented since 1925.[45]

Despite the lack of a permanent auditorium, the SSO did very well in the 1920s. A powerful board of directors and a strong auxiliary of Syracuse women managed it.[46]

Many world-famous artists played and sang with the Syracuse Symphony during this decade. Among them was a young Russian musician. The playbill for February 27, 1926, states, "Serge Prokofieff, distinguished composer and pianist, is to assist Conductor Shavitch for the seventh Symphony Concert." Robert Friedel, reviewer for the concert, wrote, "The *Concerto in C Major* was a novelty of modern composition, played by the composer himself on the piano. In it were none of the pyrotechnics, which are so often mistaken for modern progression and new ideas. Prokofieff played with brilliancy and smoothness."[47]

The now well-established and -respected SSO made its first out-of-town appearance in Watertown, New York, on October 26, 1926. A large photo of Shavitch and Tina Lerner attired in hats and long winter coats, captioned "Carrying Music to North," appeared in the local newspaper. The accompanying article read, "The SSO under Conductor Shavitch received a tremendous ovation from more than 1,000 people at Asbury ME [Methodist] Church."[48]

Shavitch continued to receive invitations to conduct the great symphonies of Europe and South America. He returned to conduct in Queen's Hall, London, several times. He conducted in Russia in 1926, 1928, and 1933; in Paris, Berlin, Dresden, and Leipzig in 1926; and in Madrid in 1927. The eighth season of the SSO ended in March 1928, to accommodate his absence.[49]

After the ninth subscription concert in March 1929, Shavitch was granted a leave of absence to enable him to head the Berlin Symphony for the balance of the season. He was the first American to hold a conducting position in the German capital. The SSO closed its season in March with the tenth subscription concert, for which Shavitch had invited Arthur Honegger, famous French composer-conductor, to lead the orchestra. It was the first time a guest conductor had appeared with the SSO since its reorganization.[50]

Financial vicissitudes and other issues of the times precipitated the slow demise of the SSO. The Great Depression of 1929 interrupted

Carrying Music to North

Uladimir Shavitch, Tina Lerner, and Harold McGrath, SSO Board member

Symphony's first out-of-town appearance in Watertown, New York, October 26, 1926.

the flow of funds needed to meet the ongoing expenses of the orchestra and other cultural organizations.

An internal dispute among the SSO board members further contributed to the downfall. At a board meeting in 1932, John Derschung (chairman), Mrs. H. Winfield Chapin (Marie Arnold), Martin Knapp, Aurin Chase (original executive board member), Mrs. Lewis Smith (Maude Mixer), and Donald S. McChesney (publisher and Onondaga Savings trustee) asked not to be renamed to their board positions.

Some executive members who relinquished their places were opposed to continuing concerts during the 1932–33 season owing to the existing business conditions.[51]

Shavitch had just hired several Rochester Philharmonic first-chair players, which angered members of the SSO as well as local patrons. Meanwhile, Shavitch continued to receive invitations to conduct on the great stages of Europe, leaving the faltering orchestra with less than sufficient leadership.

The new SSO board, however, took on the task of keeping the symphony going. Board member Mrs. A. Dudley (Gertrude Woodhall, chairman of Syracuse Salon Musicals) stated, "The Orchestra can and must be maintained. This is work for the future. We are training young people in the appreciation of the beautiful in sound." The new board proposed a tentative policy of continuing symphonic concerts for the unstable 1932–33 season. The plan was to present eight concerts for $10.00 instead of ten concerts for $12.50. No other radical changes were contemplated.[52]

Musically, it was a stunning season for the orchestra, though it lost money. Shavitch conducted the opening concert to a full auditorium, but he was on leave for the next two concerts. Returning in February 1933, he conducted a very important concert with Percy Grainger, visiting guest artist from Melbourne, Australia. The local newspaper reported, "Mr. Grainger performed his composition 'The Grainger Suite' on the piano with Mrs. Grainger playing the marimba and staff bells. For an encore he returned to play, as a pianoforte solo, the poignantly beautiful 'Lullaby' of Brahms."[53]

In May 1933 Shavitch was invited to conduct a series of concerts in Russia. A cablegram arrived from Moscow offering him fifteen concerts in Baka, Kiev, Tbilisi (Tiflis), and Moscow. It marked his fifth visit to Soviet Russia and the end of his musical leadership of the SSO.[54] Vladimir Shavitch had changed the composition of the SSO by recruiting several musicians from Rochester, brought prominent soloists to Syracuse, built subscription series of ten concerts each season, begun a "pops" series, and conducted the orchestra in other cities near Syracuse.[55] At the end of the twelfth season, in the spring of

1933, the SSO board voted to disband the organization that had once shown great promise to succeed.[56]

However, several programs followed after the formal dissolution of the first SSO. There remained a group of Syracuse citizens who would not be denied a local symphony. In the fall of 1933 Victor Miller, a pianist and conductor, was selected to lead what was to be called the Civic Symphony Orchestra. It was sponsored by the City of Syracuse and was composed of union musicians from the immediate area. Concerts under Miller began in November in the Lincoln Auditorium on Sunday afternoons. This orchestra had about sixty musicians and many guest artists and local soloists who had gained outstanding reputations in their specialized fields.[57]

André Polah followed Miller as conductor and music director from 1934 to 1938. Polah was head of the string department in the College of Fine Arts at Syracuse University and conducted the university orchestra as well.[58] Polah's orchestra flourished, especially after 1935

Victor Miller, director of the Civic Symphony Orchestra, 1933.

when it began receiving 90 percent of its operating moneys from the Works Progress Administration (WPA). The orchestra was considered a federal music project under Roosevelt's New Deal. Still operating under the original 1925 charter, it was called the Syracuse Federal Symphony. As long as the funds were available, free public concerts were presented twice each week. The first free concert was held on March 21, 1934, at the Lincoln Auditorium, and was repeated at the Onondaga Hotel's roof garden.[59]

The musicians were paid twenty-five dollars a week and the conductors forty-five dollars a week. Charles Goulding, business manager, was paid thirty dollars a week, for a total weekly payroll of seventeen hundred dollars. The Syracuse Federal Symphony was New York State's only WPA-supported symphony orchestra.[60] Alexis Muench, civil works administrator of Onondaga County, reported, "The purpose of this project is to furnish needed employment to musicians who are without work and to supply symphonic music for the public to

Professor André Polah, conductor, 1934.

enjoy." All business came under the scrutiny of Regis Luke, Syracuse supervisor-manager of the federal music project.[61]

Polah resigned in 1939 and joined Leopold Stokowski and Fritz Reiner as a coconductor of the American Lyric Theater in New York City. Around this time the WPA federal funds decreased. Francis Frank—composer, pianist, and former director of the Binghamton Symphony Orchestra—conducted the group for a brief period. After Frank died suddenly from appendicitis, Dr. Nicholas Gualillo was hired as acting conductor to finish out the 1939–40 season. Gualillo, from Utica, New York, had at one time been the assistant conductor under Polah. Gualillo reorganized the professional musicians and student musicians from the Syracuse University Orchestra into the Syracuse Civic University Symphony.[62]

On January 29, 1940, the symphony's membership met to reorganize. It changed its name to the Syracuse Symphony Orchestra Association. The members voted for the name change to end confusion between the symphony and its sponsoring organization. Frederick R. Ripley, musician and local author of *Songs for a Soldier*, was elected

Conductor Nicholas Gualillo, 1939.

president. William A. Mackensie, a practicing attorney, was elected chairman of the board. During the 1941–42 season the group successfully presented four symphony concerts, a grand opera, a light opera, and two operatic musicales in cooperation with the Onondaga Opera Association.[63]

Another symphonic group was formed in 1942, calling itself the Syracuse Philharmonic Society, "the people's symphony." It was made up of professional musicians from the local musicians union. Conductors Dr. Nicholas Gualillo and Robert Woods led the musicians for several years and into the 1950s.[64]

Concurrently, a new symphony society was launched on November 18, 1949. According to the *Syracuse Post-Standard*, it was to be the "city's own orchestra." It was called the Syracuse Symphony Orchestra, just as it was named in 1921 under the leadership of Melville Clark and William Berwald. This latest effort was spearheaded by the indefatigable Mrs. H. Winfield Chapin. Dr. Alexander Capurso, director of the School of Music at Syracuse University, was hired to be the musical director and conductor of the seventy-piece professional orchestra. Three concerts were planned for the winter season (1949–50), and a free concert for children was also scheduled—all to be held at the Lincoln Auditorium.

There was apparently always a need for more professional musical performances in Syracuse. In the 1940s and 1950s Murray Bernthal, concert pianist and violinist, organized a small group of thirty string players from Syracuse and Rochester, forming the Syracuse String Sinfonietta. They gave two or three concerts each season and featured many fine visiting soloists. They were funded by various grants secured by the music director and conductor, Bernthal. The Sinfonietta was active and very popular for several years, performing in the Lincoln Auditorium.[65]

During the 1940s and 1950s several Syracuse professional musicians performed in two or more musical organizations during the same season. The names of the organizations changed, new boards were elected, and new musical directors were hired and fired. It became apparent that a major reorganization of all the orchestral groups in Syracuse was necessary. In December 1958, three musical organizations decided to consolidate—becoming the Onondaga Symphony—for the purpose of promoting serious music in Syracuse. The Friends of Chamber Music, the Symphony Orchestra, and the Syracuse Chorale presented the first of their joint concerts on April 4, 1959. Lucas Foss was the guest conductor, soloist, and composer. In May of the same year, the concert version of *La Traviata* was presented by the same three groups.[66] That effort was rewarded by a July 1961 grant of $50,000 from the Rosamond Gifford Foundation to organize a new symphony.[67]

Thus, a new Syracuse Symphony Orchestra was founded as an outgrowth of the Onondaga Symphony. Coincidentally, it too was set in motion by a harpist, Carolyn Auth Hopkins. The present symphony remains an active and important organization in Syracuse. In 2011 it begins its fiftieth anniversary year.

7

Singing Troops and War Balloons

AS A PATRIOTIC CITIZEN during World War I, Melville A. Clark was involved in various war-related projects. Not surprisingly, one of them involved music. The other involved balloons!

Syracuse, not unlike most of the country's communities in 1917, had small opportunity to forget that the United States was at war. A huge armed camp at the New York State Fairgrounds lent a military aspect to the city. It was an achievement of ambitious business leaders who brought a two hundred thousand–dollar camp to the shores of Lake Onondaga for two summers, despite the necessity for evacuation in the cold winters. The cantonment, officially known as "Syracuse Recruitment Camp," spread from the fairgrounds for four miles on Van Vleck Road along the lakeshore known then as Pleasant Beach. About seventeen thousand men were transferred into the lakeside camp in 1917 and almost as many the next year. Railroad depots in the area were kept humming to transport the troops and supplies.[1]

Here is Clark's account of the musical project:

It was toward twilight of a dismal, rain-soaked day in 1917. I was passing by Pleasant Beach, Onondaga Lake, near Camp Onondaga, Syracuse, New York. Soldiers were standing around everywhere, with nothing in particular to do and no place to go, except, eventually, "over there." That was the sight that haunted me. I could not forget the look of those boys, just standing there, waiting and waiting for who knew what? And with nothing to pep them up and nothing to help ease the hours along.

96

Postcard of Syracuse Recruitment Camp, 1917, courtesy of the Onondaga Historical Association.

The more I thought about it, the more I knew something had to be done—something to give them a lift, something to inject in them that old football team spirit. I knew one thing that could do it was music. But it must be music they themselves could join in, not just "entertainment" from the outside.

That gave me an idea of a community chorus. With the idea came the usual obstacles. We had to solve problems of electric lights, a suitable platform, song leaders, getting a chorus together, transportation, and the always-present consideration of financing. One influential Syracuse citizen saw its worth and took care of that. Our other problems were solved as we worked, and in about four weeks, a chorus of 2,000 young women, accompanied by twelve harps, was ready to give the boys some music. Harry Barnhart was the first director and conductor.[2]

Every week, for many weeks we put on our "sings" at Camp Onondaga. How the boys loved them! The biggest hit was the "Barcarole" from Tales of Hoffman; somehow that number seemed to lend itself perfectly to the voices and harps out there under the stars.

One of the songs was, "What Are You Going To Do To Help The Boys?" Our sings at Camp Onondaga were the beginning of my opportunity to answer that question in my own experience. For soon after their inauguration, Margaret Woodrow Wilson, the President's daughter, asked me to join her troupe, then touring the camps and hospitals in the eastern part of the United States, as harp soloist and accompanist.[3] Margaret had one unquenchable ambition at that time: to sing for our boys. So thoroughly did she believe in the need for this service, that she persuaded her father to let her do it.

It was no easy trip—through New York, New Jersey, Maryland, Virginia, and West Virginia. We usually averaged four to six performances a day. One by one various members of the troupe would give up and drop out. Not Margaret. She was a real trouper.

Margaret Wilson and Melville Clark entertaining the troops at Camp May, New Jersey, in the spring of 1918.

Wherever we went, the auditoriums were filled with soldiers eager for our music. We always began the program with the little Clark Irish Harp. Margaret included among her songs the music she felt the boys would like best—"Danny Boy," "Carry Me Back to Old Virginny," and other Stephen Foster melodies. On the harp I would play different folk tunes, Irish, Scottish, Italian or Negro melodies, depending on the audience. We'd wind up with the rousing war songs of the time—"Keep the Home Fires Burning," "Long, Long Trail," "K-K-Katy," "Over There"—on which everybody sang. In that singing the boys forgot their differences, despondency, and homesickness. We could actually feel the relaxing of the tension. They were singing ten thousand as one. I shall never forget it. It is a matter of record that Napoleon ascribed his defeat in Russia to two major foes: the singing of the Russian soldiers and the severity of the Russian winter.[4]

The troupe paid their own expenses and tried to present their programs at the more isolated posts on the eastern seaboard. Following their eastern tour, Wilson's troupe entertained at the western camps. From March 24 to April 20, 1918, they gave eighteen concerts in Kansas, Oklahoma, Texas, and California.

Shortly after the United States entered World War I, Clark conceived the idea of a balloon offensive against Germany. He thought that the kaiser-led countries should be told the truth about the German warlords. His plan was to spread truthful information into enemy territory by means of message-carrying balloons. He called it the "Plan of Aerostation." After he had thoroughly researched and outlined it, he presented it to the proper authorities for approval. In August 1917 Clark was invited to discuss his plan with Ralph Pulitzer and Charles M. Lincoln, owner and editor, respectively, of the *New York World,* a New York City news daily.[5] Before going to New York he sent blueprints of the plan to his namesake, Uncle Melville Clark, in Chicago. Uncle Melville responded as follows:

The contents of the registered letter containing the blueprints were certainly a surprise. I had no idea you were working on a scheme of this magnitude. It is so hopelessly original that it is out of my power to say whether it is of value or not (and I am used to original ideas).[6] It is certainly an original scheme for disseminating news in Germany and Austria, but whether it would really reach the German people or not is the question. If the German people really knew the truth, the Emperor's head as well as the heads of his followers, would not be on his shoulders any great length of time. It is certainly to your credit to work out the scheme for its intended purpose.[7]

Pulitzer and Lincoln liked the plan and agreed to finance the project, stocking up to five hundred thousand balloons. They said Clark had to go to Washington, D.C., to get the proper authorization to continue the project. Pulitzer arranged for him to meet with the chairman of the National Advisory Committee for Aeronautics. The chairman felt Clark's plan was perfectly practical and had great value. He volunteered his staff of experts to put the plan into action.[8]

Clark's next meeting was with the head of the War College and the general staff of the U.S. Army. Clark had two sessions with each office. They discussed the practicality of using rubber or silk to make the balloons, instead of some other fabric such as court plaster. The war staff believed the rubber material of the balloons would be of no worth to the Germans, even though it was scarce. They believed that a balloon offensive into enemy territory with messages bearing the truth had great intrinsic value and might be of incalculable service in helping to end the war.[9]

After receiving approval from the War College, Clark was invited to present his idea to President Wilson. Clark recalled, "I had twenty-five minutes and he stated that he would give it earnest and careful consideration. He had many interesting things to say and questions about it. I feel that great progress has been made. It all depends upon the President now."[10]

Clark's idea of a balloon offensive appealed to the war strategists of the United States and their allies for many reasons. The German war machines would be powerless against such an offensive. If the Germans were to begin shooting down balloons, their attention would be diverted from trying to kill the Allies. Airplanes—each costing a thousand times more than the balloons—and highly trained pilots would not have to fly over enemy territory; rather, balloon-carrying messages could be guided to their destination by air currents alone.[11]

Most important would be the effect on the morale of the German people. They had been told they were winning on all fronts and that their victorious armies were invading the United States. The messages in the balloons would reinforce the doubts in their own minds. Indeed, in the fall of 1917, things were not going as well on the western front as the Germans would have expected had a victory been imminent.[12]

After Clark returned to Syracuse from his trips to New York City and Washington, D.C., he wrote an update to Uncle Melville in Chicago: "These hard headed, practical men were tremendously enthusiastic over the plan, and stated that it was the best planned strategy that had been presented and that it might be the means of saving thousands of lives. When I was asked to take it up with the Secretary of War, I finally began to realize that the plan was bigger than even I thought. The President was the most gracious and cordial person that I have ever met."[13]

With the endorsement of his idea from two of the men he respected most, President Wilson and Uncle Melville Clark, the younger Clark continued developing his secret plan. He wrote to the National Weather Bureau requesting maps showing the winds of Europe. He consulted with the local weather expert, Morgan R. Sanford, about the air currents and the topography of Germany. He learned that all of Germany, except for the most mountainous parts of the country, could be reached by flying messages. He was, however, discouraged to learn that the wind could not be counted upon to carry the balloons into the central and eastern European countries.[14]

Clark sent letters of inquiry to several balloon companies. In September 1917 he sent one to the Howe-Bauman Company, in Newark, New Jersey: "Will you kindly send samples and the best prices of your rubber balloons in thousand, ten thousand, and hundred thousand lots. We want something that will have the greatest carrying power and strength and greatest durability in the air. They are to be a foot and one half in diameter." Another letter, to the Goodyear Rubber Company in Akron, Ohio, read: "Please send information regarding specially treated silk fabric and rubber balloons which will minimize the loss of hydrogen when inflated. In other words, a balloon that would be spherical in shape of about a foot and a half in diameter. The balloon must be one that will carry as far as possible and have the greatest lifting power possible."[15]

When writing to the Miller Rubber Company in Akron Clark asked for price quotations for rubber balloons the size of watermelons. He explained, "It should contain hydrogen, the best [quality] without the self-operating valve, made in an orange color. Please state how long they would remain in the air inflated with the hydrogen gas."[16]

The first prototypes made for Clark were of rubber. Later, government officials decided that rubber would be of value to the enemy. They calculated that each balloon would furnish enough rubber for six enemy gas masks.[17] There followed experiments with paper balloons, which were chemically treated with a solution that guaranteed the retention of the hydrogen.[18] Clark began launching the experimental paper balloons from the Syracuse area. His little balloons traveled as far as Nova Scotia. Return mail cards were attached to them so that Clark could have reports of the landing places of the hydrogen-filled bags. The longest recorded flight of a balloon had been four hundred miles. But when, on August 31, 1917, a woman in Henderson, Indiana, launched one that landed about six hundred miles south in Hot Springs, Arkansas, Clark was greatly encouraged.[19]

Meanwhile, the British had been experimenting with their own devices for sending propaganda into Germany. After they heard about the newly proposed American plan, they initiated talks with Clark. Lieutenant Colonel Faunthorpe, a member of the general staff, was sent to Syracuse to meet with Clark. A demonstration was set up for his benefit. The experimental launchings so pleased Faunthorpe that he requested a sample balloon to take back to Lord Northcliffe and the British Press Bureau. Clark wrote to Lord Northcliffe concerning the meeting with Faunthorpe: "I received a call from Lieut. Col. J. C.

Faunthorpe regarding balloons which I have been experimenting with for over a year, and have now perfected for distributing propaganda. I am absolutely sure each balloon will carry messages of 1000 to 50,000 words and travel 90 to 1000 miles."[20]

Clark sent test balloons to the British. Lord Northcliffe conducted an experiment with one of the models in a garden on his own estate and gave the invention his unqualified endorsement. Other British officials soon gave the Plan of Aerostation their approval. With the permission of the United States, whose army was not then on the firing line, the plan was offered to the British.[21]

Two points particularly appealed to the British officials: the balloons had 100 percent visibility, and they were practical. After a balloon landed it would sway back and forth in the breeze; it was bound to catch someone's attention. The British liked the idea of attaching phosphorescent scales to the balloons to make them visible at night.

The first balloons were released in March 1918. Within a single week in August 1918 the British released 1.25 million balloons, each carrying a 5,000-word message. President Wilson's December 4, 1917, address on war arms was included in the message. Unguided by humans, the tiny balloons, protected from the elements by waterproof paper, were lofted into enemy territory by steady northeast winds. The German warlords were stunned at the sight of the new enemy. The balloon offensive forced the Germans into a counterstrategy of offering a reward of three to six German marks for the return of unopened messages.[22]

The Plan of Aerostation had been a carefully guarded secret. After Clark's plan won the interest of the U.S. government, he was cautioned to maintain strict secrecy while working out the details. Only the end of the war made it possible for the people of Syracuse to learn the name of the mastermind of the plan. The following were some of the headlines in the Syracuse newspapers: "War Balloon Move Planned by Melville Clark," "Idea of Sending Millions of Pamphlets into Germany Originated with Piano Man," "Syracuse Man's Genius Means of Carrying Allied Propaganda over German Lines," and "Clark Credited with Deadly Balloon Offensive."[23]

BRITISH SOLDIERS PREPARING TO BOMBARD GERMAN FIRST-LINE MORALE
WITH PROPAGANDA. (© *Western Newspaper U*

Clipping from Clark materials of British soldiers with propaganda balloons.

Clark simply called the balloon offensive "proof of practicality." Certainly, the balloon offensive helped to shatter the morale of the kaiser's troops in the last months of World War I. Military historians claim that if Clark had been a British citizen, the queen would have knighted him.

8

White House Connections

FOR A MUSICIAN to be invited to play at the White House is a great honor. Melville Clark recalled his performances there for Presidents Wilson, Harding, and Roosevelt with clarity and pride.

Clark's first invitation to play at the White House came because of his association with John McCormack, one of the most popular tenors of the time. McCormack always made a stop at the Clark Music store when he was performing in upstate New York. On one of his visits he bought a Clark Irish Harp for his child. He was so impressed with the instrument that he invited its maker to join him on a series of tours that lasted two years.

On March 27, 1914, during one of these tours, Clark first performed at the White House along with McCormack and other musicians. That evening he met the president's eldest daughter, Margaret, a lyric soprano, who also performed for the guests.[1]

Two months later, on May 27, 1914, he made a return visit to the White House to accompany Margaret Wilson on the harp. For this performance he played two solos on the concert harp and a medley of Irish melodies on the Clark Irish Harp. The musicale for five hundred distinguished guests was preceded by a dinner for friends and family of the president, members of the diplomatic corps, and cabinet members. The president's daughter assisted with the entertainment arrangements, owing to the failing health of Mrs. Wilson. Clark was one of eight recipients to receive a gold medal by executive order that evening.[2]

A week later, on June 3, 1914, a thank-you letter from Mrs. Wilson's secretary was sent to Clark. It read, "Mrs. Wilson was unable to be in the East Room for the musicale, but she enjoyed it all from the upper floor and your playing gave her so much pleasure. She is sending you a memento of the occasion, a pin, which she hopes you will accept. Isabelle Hapices, Secy." The pin was in the shape of a lyre called the harp of Orpheus, with the U.S. seal in relief. The significance of the design was that Clark had played "Orpheus" on the concert harp at the musicale. The token came as a surprise to Clark, who said, "I am far more proud of it than if it had been a jeweled decoration from a European monarch." Ellen Axson Wilson, America's first lady, died on August 6, 1914.[3]

These events were memorable for Clark—so much so that he wrote an essay for the *Christian Science Monitor*'s May 19, 1945, issue titled, "I Played the Harp for Wilson." The piece read as if he had been there yesterday. The last paragraphs foreshadowed the difficult times that lay ahead for the president:

> When the last distinguished guest had departed, the president asked me to take the harp and go with him to the rear portico of the White House. It afterward became plain that he was gravely worried over the possibilities of war between the United States and the countries of the diplomats he had just entertained; and sought to relieve the tension by singing.
>
> I was counting it a great privilege, as well as a pleasure, to be able to give the president a lift at a time when he was burdened perhaps with the melancholy thought that his guests, that evening, might soon be his mortal enemies. But I assumed he wished merely to sit awhile in the soft May time air and listen to the harp.
>
> He asked me if I could play "Drink to Me Only With Thine Eyes" and I bent eagerly over the harp and began softly the familiar melody. Then I was surprised when the president began to sing the song in a clear lyric tenor voice.
>
> He suggested one song after another—Scottish and Irish songs and those of Stephen Foster. He sang easily and with faultless diction. It was nearly midnight when he stood up to go, amazingly buoyant, relaxed and unworried.[4]

Clark and Miss Margaret Wilson became fast friends and cor-
responded with each other on a regular basis. He encouraged her
to begin a musical singing career, something she had always wanted
to do after years of vocal lessons. In 1915 Clark invited Wilson to
make her public debut appearance during the popular Central New
York Music Festival, of which he was secretary for twelve years. The
festival was an annual five-day celebration of concerts. It drew great
audiences from a large area to hear the most celebrated vocalists, solo
instrumentalists, and symphonies of the time. The Chicago Symphony (1915), the New York City Metropolitan Opera Symphony,
the Cleveland Symphony (1923), and the Boston Symphony (1913
and 1920) all traveled to Syracuse to be on the festival programs.
When Wilson accepted his invitation to participate, Clark was exu-
berant. It was reported in the local newspapers that her debut caused
a social flurry in Syracuse.

A luncheon at the 500 Club hosted by Melville A. Clark during the music
festival, May 1915, in Syracuse. *Left to right:* Melville A. Clark, Mrs. William
Hitz (wife of the supreme court judge of the District of Columbia), Marion
Davis, and Margaret Woodrow Wilson.

On May 12, 1915, sixty-two hundred persons jammed the Arena Auditorium to see and hear Wilson at the closing performance of the festival. The local newspaper reported:

> The Arena was thronged with curiosity seekers. Outside the traffic was at a standstill and the opening of the concert was delayed to permit the late arrivers to obtain their seats. A special squad of Syracuse police had to be sent to the scene to handle the crush of onlookers. Arriving on the stage, she was presented a huge box of roses, sent by the president from the White House. Being the president's daughter, she overshadowed the other principals such as Conductor Dr. Frederick Stock and the [participating] Chicago Symphony, Frances Alda, Pasquale Amato and Katherine Goodman, the reigning concert stars of the day. She received a $1000 fee for her appearance here and made the Music Festival a $2009 profit, one of the few times the event paid its own way. Miss Wilson donated her fee to two institutions for the blind in Washington DC.

Clark said in retrospect, "Miss Wilson did not have a great voice but she had superb self-confidence and training. She was completely at home on the stage."[5]

Another important American in the audience that evening was a former president, Theodore Roosevelt, in Syracuse to work on a libel suit.[6] "Colonel Roosevelt was in Syracuse to testify in his defense for a $50,000 libel suit brought against him by William Barnes, ex-chairman of the New York State Republican Committee. Roosevelt libeled Barnes as a political boss of the most obnoxious type, attempting to sully his good name and reputation. The trial was held at the Onondaga County Court House, which was deemed to be a more neutral site than court houses in Albany or New York City."[7]

The president's daughter and Melville Clark continued their friendship through letters and postcards. Syracuse University Library's Special Collections Research Center has more than sixty letters from Miss Wilson to Clark sent from the White House between 1914 and 1921. A letter penned by Wilson to Clark on May 15, 1914, began, "My dear Mr. Clarke," and ended, "Sincerely Yours." The last name was

The Wilson party at the door of the auditorium preceding the concert, May 1915, Syracuse. *Left to right:* Elizabeth David, accompanist; Ross David, voice teacher; Margaret Woodrow Wilson; Marion Davis, traveling companion; and Melville A. Clark.

misspelled and had a formal salutation and closing. But by February 28, 1916, the penned letter began, "My dear boy," and closed with, "Ever your devoted friend." It was a thank-you letter for the violets Clark had sent her a week before.[8]

Clark and his sister Maude performed on their concert harps at the White House on January 25, 1916. It was the last embassy dinner held by the Wilsons before the United States entered World War I, during which all diplomatic dinners and musicales were suspended. It was reported in the *Washington Times* that, for that dinner, the president's second wife, Edith Galt Wilson, wore one of the handsomest toilettes in her trousseau. The German ambassador was the ranking guest, and envoys of the Central powers and representatives of the neutral nations made up the party of sixty.[9]

In 1918 Clark, with his portable Clark Irish Harp, was invited to become a member of Margaret Wilson's troupe, entertaining the soldiers at military camps throughout the country (see chapter 3). In addition to Wilson and Clark, the little troupe included Elizabeth and Ross David of New York City, who were Wilson's piano accompanist and voice coach, respectively. A typical tour lasted three to four weeks. For the first two weeks they entertained at the army encampments, and for the last two weeks they arranged concerts along the way to defray the expenses incurred performing for the troops.[10]

Melville and Margaret continued to correspond after the Wilson White House years. Miss Wilson moved to New York City and became part of the labor force. In 1923 she wrote, "I have gone into the advertising business because I want to support myself without any delay." The letter was written on stationery from the Biow

Margaret Wilson rehearsing for the fall concerts at Cornish, New Hampshire. *Left to right:* Melville A. Clark, harpist; Wilson; Elizabeth David, accompanist; and Ross David, voice teacher. *Musical America,* October 15, 1915, 12.

Company, an advertising agency in New York.[11] There is no record of their performing together again after World War I.

In 1938 Margaret Wilson left the United States to become part of the Sri Aurobindo Ashram in Pondicherry, India. She became a recluse, seeking refuge from a troubled world. She never returned home and died in India in 1944.

Exactly twenty-one years after his first White House debut, Melville Clark found himself performing in the White House again at the invitation of President and Mrs. Franklin D. Roosevelt. Henry Junge of the Steinway Company had been entrusted with the details of the White House programs for twenty-five years. Junge began when Taft was president and continued this service through the terms of Wilson, Harding, Coolidge, Hoover, and Franklin D. Roosevelt. The letter of April 30, 1935, on Steinway stationery, reads as follows:

> Dear Mr. Clark:
>
> It affords me great pleasure to inform you that Mrs. Franklin D. Roosevelt will be delighted to have you play a harp program at a White House Musicale after a Dinner given by the president and Mrs. Roosevelt to Governor Lehman [New York State] on May 15, 1935.
>
> I trust that your engagements will permit you to grace this occasion with your artistry and charming presence.
>
> The Manhattan String Quartette will share the program, consisting of 2 groups. After the first group of the Quartette, it is suggested, that you play your Harp numbers, having a duration of about 12 minutes, followed by the Quartette's second group, which will close the program.
>
> You are, of course, most competent in the choice of your numbers for your part of the program, but I venture to suggest the avoidance of too many classical compositions; they like them melodious and joyful.
>
> I am charmed to be the harbinger and intermediary of this gladsome news and with kind regards, believe me,
>
> Cordially yours,
> Henry Junge[12]

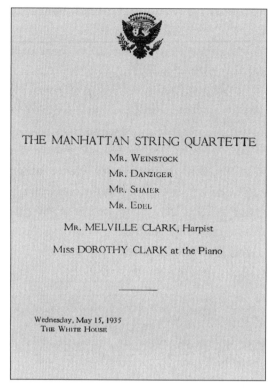

THE MANHATTAN STRING QUARTETTE

Mr. WEINSTOCK

Mr. DANZIGER

Mr. SHAIER

Mr. EDEL

Mr. MELVILLE CLARK, Harpist

Miss DOROTHY CLARK at the Piano

———

Wednesday, May 15, 1935
THE WHITE HOUSE

White House Musicale program.

Clark not only brought the concert harp and the Clark Irish Harp to the White House, but he also brought his wife, Dorothy, to accompany him on the piano. They performed for ninety-three guests in the family dining room.[13] Perhaps it helped him to win a place in the Roosevelts' hearts, as he and Dorothy were invited to attend all ceremonies pertaining to the inauguration of President Roosevelt's second term on January 20, 1937.[14]

Clark played again for the Roosevelts. But his most memorable Washington experience was the evening he played alone for President Wilson on the eve of World War I, on a little portico at the rear of the White House.

9

The Collections

HUMAN BEINGS collect things. The small boy begins by filling his pockets and the little girl her secret treasure box. Some people outgrow the habit. Others, who fancy an item really worthwhile, continue to pick up better and better pieces until they have accumulated a considerable "collection." Melville Clark had three famous collections: antique music boxes, antique harps, and rare musical instruments. His early gramophone or phonograph collection became part of Syracuse University's Audio Archive (now the Belfer Audio Laboratory and Archive).

Stamp Collection

Clark began to be an enthusiastic stamp collector when he was about five. He was too young to read but was fascinated with the occasional envelopes that came from abroad, addressed to his father. He would pull the impressive-looking envelopes out of the wastebasket to look at the colorful stamps.

In his lifetime he amassed some thirty-five thousand stamps from almost every country in the world. He organized the collection and put some in cellophane envelopes, while mounting many hundreds of the rare items in proper stamp albums.[1]

Because of his close association with the harp, Clark made a special effort to secure stamps from countries that used the harp image on their stamps. There exist today nineteen perfectly preserved harp-imprinted stamps on a page that was most likely separated from its album when the collection was sold. Five are from Eire (Ireland), four from New South Wales (Australia), three from Estonia, three from

Italy, one from Russia, and three from Montserrat (one of the Leeward Islands in the British West Indies). He collected the harp-imprinted stamps over a period of twenty-five years.[2] The bulk of the stamp collection was sold to a dealer during Clark's lifetime; it was not famous, but it did bring a substantial price to the collector.

Early Phonograph Collection

Melville A. Clark's collection of twenty-eight early and historic phonographs and gramophones was viewed by most of the Clark Music Company store's clients on a regular basis. They were displayed on the fifth floor in the antique room. There were Edisons, Victors, Reginaphones, Columbias, and Berliners along with seventeen thousand records. His friend Walter L. Welch also collected early machines and records.[3] Their combined historic collections, the Clark-Welch Collection, became part of Syracuse University's Audio Archive. Welch, the original curator of the archive from 1963 to 1991, was a nationally recognized authority on the history of recorded sound. Some of the early machines are still on view at the Belfer Audio Laboratory and Archive, which has grown to be the fourth-largest such archive in the United States, according to a current staff member.[4] Clark wrote an article for the *Christian Science Monitor,* dated December 14, 1946, in which he delineated the history of the recording industry from 1877 to the present. He called it "Captured Sound," explaining the huge contribution that recorded speech and music could make to our present and future world of music and to our cultural resources.

Music Box Collection

When Henry Ford was assembling antiques for his famous Edison Institute in Dearborn, Michigan, he hired Melville Clark as a "picker." Ford would tell Clark about an item he wanted for his collection, and Clark would set off looking for it. He picked up antiques and appointed eleven pickers to assist him. Clark said, "Maybe it would be a straight-line engine, maybe a salt-box house. Syracuse, N.Y., was famous for salt houses.[5] So, when I was no longer needed to pick up

Walter Welch and Melville A. Clark holding early recordings from their collection, 1951.

things for Mr. Ford, I developed an ardent hobby, with the same 11 pickers, of collecting music boxes." He was particularly interested in the American music box rather than the Swiss music box. The notable difference is that the American one is a disc player, using flat fifteen-inch discs; the Swiss one uses a cylinder.[6]

Clark assembled one of the best collections of American music boxes in the world. He owned sixty-eight of them and restored each one to prime condition. His collection was displayed at the Syracuse Museum of Fine Arts in December 1947. In three weeks twenty thousand people viewed the exhibit and listened to the music boxes.[7] This type of music box, popular around the 1890s, was decorated with marquetry, the ancient and all-but-forgotten art of wood inlay. The beautiful scrollwork and colored designs adorning these boxes were done by skilled craftsmen more than 150 years ago.[8]

Clark recalled, "This [successful exhibition] gave me the idea that people loved the quality of the sound of the music boxes." Clark loved telling his story about a music box, two princesses, and a harp. "Now, one particular box stood out above all others. It was perfectly made and had a perfect tone. This [music box] was a piece of mechanism over sixty years old, but it was as good as if it were brand new. I tried to think of who would get the greatest enjoyment out of this. I thought of Great Britain because few American music boxes ever got out of the States, I am told. I found the people I queried didn't even know what an American music box was—they thought it was a jukebox."[9]

The music box he referred to was a rare Regina music box, made in Rahway, New Jersey, in the 1890s. Clark had acquired it for his collection in 1930. He thought it would make a fine gift not only to Great Britain but also to the newly married Princess Elizabeth and Prince Philip, who were wed on November 20, 1947.[10]

He chose thirty-six discs to be played on the Regina. Clark said, "I found thirty-six in my own forty-year-old collection forgotten. The records [discs] were in perfect condition."

On February 2, 1948, Clark wrote to John Colville, private secretary to Her Royal Highness Princess Elizabeth, and offered her the music box. It was declined because King George had issued orders that the royal couple could not accept gifts from private individuals. They had already received thirty-five hundred gifts. The idea was dropped.[11] A week later, however, a letter from Buckingham Palace arrived addressed to "Melville Clark Esq., Syracuse, New York."

> Sir,
>
> I have shewn your letter of the 3rd February to The Princess Elizabeth and Her Royal Highness desires me to say that she will have much pleasure in accepting the musical box which you so kindly offer as a Wedding Present.
>
> The Princess thought it most kind of you to wish to give her such a delightful present.
>
> Yours truly,
>
> John Colville, Private Secretary to The Princess Elizabeth

DISCS FOR THE REGINA MUSIC BOX PRESENTED TO THE PRINCESS ELIZABETH

Section of Cabinet	Title	Words Found in "America Sings" Page Number
1	Aloha oe' Aloha de' Song	89
	Auld Lang Syne	12
2	Ben Boldt Song	47
	Blue Danube Waltz	78
3	Coming Thro' the Rye	32
	Darkie's Dream, The	
4	Directorate March, The	
	Glow-Worm, The	
5	God Save the Queen	
	Hall Columbia	108
6	Hands Across the Sea	
	Hote Time in the Old Town Tonight, A	
7	Invitation to the Dance	
	Jingle Bells	122
8	Kathleen Mavourneen, Irish Song	66
	La Paloma	
9	Merry Widow Waltz	92
	My Wild Irish Rose	
10	My Old Kentucky Home	21
	Narcissus Song	
11	Nest of Finches, A	
	Old Black Joe	14
12	On the Banks of the Wabash Far Away	
	Onward Christian Soldiers	111
13	Silent Night, Holy Night	115
	Soldiers Chorus from Faust	
14	Spinn, Spinn	
	Swanee River - Old Folks at Home	15
15	Sweetest Story Ever Told, The	
	Tell Me Pretty Maiden	
16	Tenting Tonight on the Old Camp Ground	
	Then You'll Remember Me from The Bohemian Girl	
17	Toreadore Song, The, from Carmen	
	Washington Post	
18	When the Coons have a Dreamland of Their Own Song	
	Jipp I Addy I Ay Song	

List of discs for the music box presented to Princess Elizabeth in honor of her wedding, 1948.

Knowing he had little chance of making a personal presentation to the princess because of strict rules against royalty receiving gifts personally, Clark wrote to Colville and asked permission to show the secretary how to operate the music box. He was informed that the

BUCKINGHAM PALACE

10th February, 1948.

Sir,

I have shewn your letter of the 3rd February to The Princess Elizabeth and Her Royal Highness desires me to say that she will have much pleasure in accepting the musical box which you so kindly offer as a wedding Present. The Princess thought it most kind of you to wish to give her such a delightful present.

Yours truly,

John Colville

Private Secretary to
The Princess Elizabeth.

Melville Clark Esq.,
Syracuse,
New York.

Letter from Princess Elizabeth's secretary, John Colville, from Buckingham Palace, February 10, 1948.

secretary would receive him at the palace, implying no personal audience with the princess.[12]

The rare Regina music box was set into a solid mahogany cabinet with boxwood inlay. Together, the ensemble stood four feet high. The music box itself was twenty-one inches long, nineteen inches wide, and twelve inches high. Inside the lid of the cabinet, Clark had applied the royal crest of Princess Elizabeth. This particular American music box could project three or four times the volume of a Swiss music box, and each disc played three times longer than one of the cylinders.[13]

Despite their age, the thin metal records were in perfect condition. The playing mechanism involved perforations cut into the edge of the discs. The music box had a double steel comb with a delicate star wheel between the comb teeth, which created a lovely tone when it came in contact with the perforations of the rotating disc. The box could play for thirty minutes when wound to its maximum.[14]

Officials at RCA Victor, in New York City, had heard about the music box being shipped to London. They made a proposal for recording the

Clark with Regina music box, cabinet, and discs.

discs before the music box left the United States. An appointment was set for testing the records in a Masterworks studio on April 9, 1948. The test was successful, and RCA recorded thirteen of the thirty-six available discs, to put on ten-inch record masters. A formal contract was signed later, on May 27, between RCA and Melville Clark.[15]

A special trunk was built to protect the precious cargo: the music box and its cabinet, a stand, and a second cabinet for the discs. On the morning of April 12, Clark—with the Regina music box, thirty-six discs, and a Clark Irish Harp—arrived at La Guardia Field. The harp accompanied him because he had an engagement to appear before the London Rotary Club as soloist and guest artist during his visit to England.[16] In the airport he entertained overseas travelers with an impromptu recital on the harp. Clark explained to his audience that he was anxious to try his harp on the way to London to discover whether high altitudes had any effect on the instrument and the nylon strings he had recently produced. An American Overseas Airline spokesman said the plane would fly at an altitude of seventeen thousand feet or higher. Clark reported, "As the noontime crowd of travelers and airport employees gathered, I was asked to continue to demonstrate my Clark Irish Harp. I willingly obliged and played several popular songs. The recital was ended only by the plane's departure."[17]

Once airborne Clark discovered that the American Overseas Airliner "hummed" in the key of E. When the plane climbed above twenty thousand feet, he expected the engines would probably change their tune, hopefully, he said, "to a C or an A—more restful. The plane carried about sixty passengers. At the front there was plenty of room. I sat there and struck up a popular air on the harp and was delighted to find the whole crowd chiming in."[18]

Clark was invited to arrive at Buckingham Palace at eleven thirty in the morning. He strapped the music box trunk to the rear of a large sedan, provided by American Overseas Airlines. After arriving at the palace, the trunk was unloaded and then unpacked in the private office of Secretary Colville, who was to receive instructions from Clark in how to operate the antique music box.[19]

Clark amuses the plane crew with his Irish harp, en route to London, April 13, 1948. Courtesy of the *Syracuse Herald-Journal*.

Clark arriving at Buckingham Palace with the Regina music box.

"I took the first piece out—the music box itself," said Clark, "and put it on the table in front of Mr. Colville. After I switched on the mechanism to play 'Hands Across the Sea,' immediately palace denizens and staff members came into the room, including the king's private secretary, Princess Margaret Rose, two ladies-in-waiting, stenographers, and several Scotland Yard men. They were so delighted that Mr. Colville carried the box into the hall, which was a block long and carpeted in red. Princess Elizabeth's apartment was at the end of it. Suddenly, she came out, wearing a fur cape, as she was dressed to attend a ceremony." Clark recalled, "I was introduced by her secretary," Clark recalled, "and the princess stretched out her hand—I held it extra long—and I said, 'Your Royal Highness, I'm delighted to meet you,' and I gave her a salaam." Clark reported:

> The group had been serious and austere, but immediately after they heard the next disc, the atmosphere changed. The piece was "Yip I Addy I Ay." It transformed an austere group into a gay party. The Great Hall, where the stand was placed, leads to both Princesses' rooms. This hall is filled with magnificent antiques of all kinds, and the little music box stood in the midst of them. Her Royal Highness expressed joy at the gift. What pleased the princess most was the old tune "God Save the Queen," recorded about sixty-two years earlier for her great-great-grandmother, Queen Victoria.

She thanked Clark for the wedding present. "It was a thrill," Clark exclaimed, "to have an unexpected audience with Her Royal Highness as I played her favorite tunes on the music box."[20]

Clark also recalled:

> Then someone spied my harp. Princess Margaret, seventeen years old, wanted to hear it. I played, and the party assembled for a little while. It was a special harp, [which could play] sixty-two notes, equipped with new nylon strings. I played an American tune, "Home On The Range." Princess Margaret sat down at the harp and someone suggested, "Why not take the harp to the music room?" I spent an hour with Princess Margaret and gave her a lesson. Before she

was done, she was picking out "Silent Night" with two fingers and "God Save The King" while I was adding the accompaniment on the low strings.[21]

In notes for a lecture later in 1948 Clark remembered:

It occurred to me that the harp might bring joy to Princess Margaret, so I offered it to her. She gracefully accepted. "I'll have to borrow it from you as I have a concert to give at the Rotary tomorrow," I told her. "I will bring it back with me right after the concert and show you the book of instructions I have written. I can arrange a teacher for you." "Oh, no," came the reply, "I can learn to play by myself with your lesson book. It would be fun." The seventeen-year-old Princess Margaret was an accomplished pianist and grasped the idea of playing the harp right away.[22]

The next day was the bestowing of the Order of the Garter. When Clark returned to Buckingham Palace with the harp, both princesses were away, but he was asked to personally place the Clark Irish Harp in Princess Margaret's suite. Clark said, "The room was filled with figurines and mahogany furniture, and was sunny and bright. The harp and the music box have their place in Buckingham Palace."[23]

On returning to Syracuse, Clark found a letter waiting for him from the palace, written by one of Princess Margaret's ladies-in-waiting. She stated that her royal highness was enchanted with the harp. She also wished to convey the princess's sincere gratitude for the delightful present and her thanks for the interesting lesson he gave her that day. There was also a letter from John Colville, who wrote, "The music box is still playing very merrily, and so, I feel sure, is the harp."[24]

Melville Clark had no doubt that "music hath charms," for it had offered him an audience with Princess Elizabeth in Buckingham Palace. Clark's present was one of thousands of gifts for the royal couple, but it was the only music box.[25]

Eight months after the event in Buckingham Palace, Syracuse was introduced to its first live television broadcast from the studio at the Syracuse Meredith Television Company. Melville Clark became the first guest personage on WHEN. Seated next to a basket of flowers and a gray backdrop, he discussed his recent visit to London with William Bohen, staff announcer, at 8:32 p.m. on November 30, 1948. Two inexperienced cameramen were challenged when Clark and Bohen left their seats and walked over to one of Clark's prized music boxes and played "Home Sweet Home." Then the presenters went to Clark's Irish Harp. The musician played "Drink to Me Only with Thine Eyes" and "Home on the Range," the two pieces requested by the princess during his impromptu audience.[26]

The famous music box collection comprised not only the Swiss- and American-made boxes but also hundreds of discs. For just one type of music box, the Regina, Clark had made a list of 132 discs available to play. The collection was displayed in the antique room on the fifth floor of the Clark Music Company, along with the early phonograph collection.

Gustaf Schirmer of the publishing house in New York City was looking for just such a collection. The Melville Clark music box collection was the finest he had found, and the most valuable and comprehensive. Schirmer was interested not in selling them but in adding to his growing collection in Manhattan. The music boxes would occupy a hallowed spot in his museum of instruments that he kept in the business rooms for clients to enjoy. A newspaper writer at the time described the display arranged for Schirmer's inspection: "What an array! Exquisite tiny ones to huge behemoth sizes. There were cases and boxes with intricate inlaid designs, which must have taken years to carve and fashion. The repertoire of the collection would take pages to catalogue. The tunes comprise opera, folk songs, waltzes, and popular ditties. All the best loved tunes of a former day."[27] After viewing the entire lot, Schirmer bought twenty-one pieces from the collection. A fine catalog was published with a photograph and a description of each music box. The grouping was called the Schirmer-Clark Collection of Rare Music Boxes.

After the death of Melville Clark in 1953, Walter L. Welch purchased the remainder of the Clark music boxes. He was Clark's long-time loyal friend and knew that Clark wanted to keep the collection together. It was said that he took out a personal loan for the purchase. At the time Welch was the director of Syracuse University's Audio Archive, and he anticipated that the university would purchase the collection. However, the university decided not to buy the music box collection, and in 1962 Welch divided it. Duplicate boxes and ones that were deemed not basic to the main collection were sold to the former Music Museum in Deansboro, New York. The remainder of the collection was sold to Donald House, a Syracuse resident, who had already started his own collection of old and unusual musical instruments. House bought twenty-nine of the beautiful boxes in 1963 from Welch and continues to keep them maintained and in good working order today.[28]

Antique Musical Instrument Collection

In 1948 Clark had 114 instruments in his collection, which included the harp collection. It also included the music boxes and the early American-made keyboard instruments. Each instrument had something unique about it—be it age, provenance, size, or country of origin.

Clark explained why he collected certain pieces: "those that mark a part of the development of the respective instruments and those that are playable.[29] The special items that I collect are those which mark epochs in a development of a certain instrument leading up to a modern one so as to show growth. Only instruments that are important to that development are of interest to me."[30]

He gave many lectures, always using several of the instruments to demonstrate a point. He was well known for these lectures and always in demand by civic and educational groups.

Included in one of his lists of instruments were six autophones, twelve zithers, six accordions, and a seraphin, which was an example of the first reed organ, invented in England in 1833. It had one pedal, which operated the bellows to raise the keyboard to give a "jitterbug" effect.[31] Also noted was an antique six-octave spinet piano, made by H. W. Geib; a lap piano, genesis of the square piano made in Philadelphia; and a rocker organ made in Concord, New Hampshire. Rocker organs were used at a time when organs were not allowed in churches.

A lap piano being played.

One placed it on one's lap and pumped with one's outstretched elbows while fingering the keys. Quite a trick!

In addition to the lap piano, there was also a lap organ, an American-made reed instrument that was played with push buttons. It was used in colonial churches where formerly a pitch pipe had been used to give a key to hymns. After Clark had searched for thirty-six years for this type of instrument, Estey Organ Company presented one to Clark as a gift. Clark also had in his collection two organs that had wooden cylinders with pins that strike a little metal piece that opens up the reed and thus plays a tone. He had twelve melodeons; several pianos; an antique 250-year-old bassoon having three keys versus the usual twenty-two; a yellow flute, a one-keyed instrument used before the Civil War; an Italian barrel organ; and a hurdy-gurdy, predecessor to the violin. (The name is commonly misapplied to the street piano.) Also noted was a glass harmonica, popular in the eighteenth century, and a musical chair that played "Tea for Two" or perhaps "The Bridal March" when you sat upon it. There were scores of historical drums, two from the War of 1812, and one that was used at Lincoln's funeral. There were cellos, a Hawaiian guitar, a Russian balalaika, a theramin, and violins. The smallest violin was 1/64th of the regular size. It was perfect in all details, and Clark always took it to his musical lectures.[32]

Also in the collection was an instrument Clark called a harmonium, a portable organ from Bombay (now Mumbai) used in all Hindu temples. Religious chants were recited to the music of the harmonium. It was a gift from a friend who had traveled to India.[33]

Clark, playing a lap organ, posed between the Irish harp and the Cleopatra's harp, around 1946.

There were instruments that even Clark might have had trouble pronouncing and playing, such the "gusli," an ancient dulcimer from Russia; the "pusanche," a Buryat-Mongolian stringed instrument; and the "kobus," a Kirghizian stringed instrument. Friends traveling in foreign countries brought back these unusual pieces for Clark to add to his famous assortment of musical finds.[34]

Another oddity in the collection was a "stagecoach" violin case. It was said to have been made by Stradivarius. It was constructed of end wood that would not splinter. If the violin case were thrown out of the coach and run over, the violin would not be damaged in any way.[35]

Clark's antique musical instrument collection was well known. During his lectures he always included demonstrations of many of these oddities. The collection was on display in the Clark Music store. They were all in excellent playing condition and maintained by Melville A. Clark. He added to the collection throughout the years and occasionally sold pieces to interested buyers around the world.

Harp Collection

"Harp Shown in Syracuse Was Once the Property of Famous French Queen" read a June 30, 1906, headline from the *Syracuse Post-Standard*. The Clark Music Company had this distinctive item displayed at the Clark Music store. It was one of fourteen harps that supposedly had been owned and played by Marie Antoinette, the wife of France's ill-fated King Louis XVI. After the royal family was swept from the palace at Versailles in 1789, the harp was lost. It ended up in the hands of the queen's former teacher. From there it passed to the Kendallbeck family, who brought it to the United States and settled in Ithaca. Architect William H. Miller bought it at an estate sale and eventually sold it to the Clarks.

Jean-Henri Naderman in Paris made the French harp around 1770. It was made of highly polished mahogany-like wood, exquisitely carved, with a rose and ribbon design. Regardless of whether it was actually owned by Marie Antoinette, it was called the Marie Antoinette harp to distinguish it from similar harps of the period. An interesting feature of its construction was that it had seven pedals, and it had hooks instead of wheels for the making of sharps, one semitone. The tuning pins were hand wrought, and no two were alike. All were of a different size and tapered, so as to fit the individual key exactly.[36]

When Henry Ford was assembling early musical instruments for the Edison Institute in Dearborn, Michigan, Melville Clark offered the French harp to him, as Clark was an ardent admirer of Ford. Clark had already been offered a large sum of money for the harp from artist and photographer Rodman Wanamaker, son of the Philadelphia store owner. Ford was anxious to find an authentic historic harp in perfect condition and playable. This point was an absolute condition laid down by Ford for all the antiques, whether purchased or donated to his collection. Every object had to be not only in absolutely perfect condition but also as usable for its purpose as it was in the period when it was in actual use. Ford was pleased to add the harp to his instrument collection.[37]

Years later Clark recalled his visit with Henry Ford, the day he brought the harp to the Edison Institute:

> Here we are, in the year of our Lord, [June 7] 1929, met together in the ballroom of this great building. Where in a delightful informal little ceremony, he accepted from me a gift for his Dearborn Museum, the little priceless 18th-century harp.
>
> Ford asked me to play some old Irish tunes on it and later played the same tunes on a modern harp so he could compare that with the antique. "Mr. Clark," he said, "will you play something for me on that beautiful old harp; could you play St Patrick's Day in the Morning? You know I was born in Cork." The kindly eyes twinkled at my surprise. I played the old tune and there was Henry Ford dancing a jig with all the gusto of a lad of the streets dancing to the music of a street piano.
>
> The photographers came in and he said, "Now Mr. Clark, we'll pose for posterity: I am accepting this antique harp for my collection; you are giving it to me; you are pleased; I am grateful; that's the way we must look when the picture is taken."[38]

Clark presenting a French harp to Henry Ford at the Edison
Institute, Dearborn, Michigan, 1929.

Clark's harp assemblage was probably his most valuable collection.
He owned antique harps from all parts of the world, and from the
first century BC to the 1950s. Besides France, he had obtained harps
from all the countries in the United Kingdom, the South Sea Islands,
Ethiopia, Congo, Egypt, and Russia. When United Artists Film Studio needed an authentic harp for the filming of *Caesar and Cleopatra*
in 1946, they rented Clark's "Cleo" harp. The studio also used it for

display in all the key city-spectacular openings. It was a rare harp, made in the style of an instrument called the nebal that was played in Egypt at the time of the great pharaohs, as depicted by authentic paintings on the walls of the tombs still visible today in the tomb of Ramses III and nobleman Nakht. It had ten strings and was adorned with many Egyptian symbols—the falcon's head, a lotus blossom impaled on an elephant's tusk, and an etched picture of the Nile in recession with the pyramids in the background.[39]

Clark with the Cleopatra harp, used for publicity for a movie, 1946.

There were several famous Irish harps in the collection. One of the small Irish harps Clark believed had belonged to the noted composer Thomas Moore. It is possible that Moore composed some of his ballads on this instrument. Clark had purchased it while he was in Ireland in 1905, and he said it was this harp that inspired him to design his small and inexpensive Clark Irish Harp.[40]

The oldest Irish harp in the collection was similar to the one Moore immortalized in "Harp of Tara's Hall." It was made of genuine bog oak. The decorations on the sounding board and fore pillar are letters of the Irish alphabet intertwined with Viking symbols, an art form owing to the influence of the Norse invasions into Ireland. It was the type of harp that minstrels carried when wandering through the countryside. With its accompaniment, they would announce the news of the times—political, religious, and general information that would interest the folks of the area. Clark said these singers were the newsmongers of that period.[41]

He also acquired the famous Irish patriot Robert Emmet's own Irish harp, built by Egan in Dublin. Clark purchased it from Emmet's descendants and received documents attesting to its authenticity. It measured thirty-six inches high, twenty-two inches deep, and eight inches wide. It had thirty strings and six sound holes. There were seven thumb-action levers on the pillar to make a change of keys, and they were linked like a modern harp with movable discs. It was this harp that Robert Emmet used to get the attention of the people during his political campaign before the British hanged him in Ireland on September 20, 1803. He was found guilty of appealing (unsuccessfully) to Emperor Napoléon Bonaparte for French aid and for leading an insurrection in Dublin.[42]

At the time that Clark was establishing his harp collection, he was studying the history of the harp of each country. When he was delving into the history of the harp in China, he noticed mention of a pigeon harp or whistle, of which he had never heard before. Clark contacted friends in China in an effort to obtain one, and he was sent five of these little harps from George R. Merrell of Harbin,

Manchuria. He was the American consul to China. The Manchurian dove harp is really a small Aeolian harp, played by the wind. It is a very small instrument, one-half ounce—so small it could be held in the hand and affixed to carrier pigeons. It is made up of tiny pipes, three inches long by two inches wide. They are made of very fine wood, lighter than cork, and they attach to the leg of a pigeon. The pipes are all differently tuned to produce a harmonious tone when the bird flies swiftly. Frightened by the sound of the pipes, the birds would fly faster and faster. Upon hearing these sounds, the pigeons, believing there was an enemy in pursuit, would fly great distances to get away from it. Thus, racing and homing pigeons were trained to stay in the air for many miles without a stop.[43]

A tiny Manchurian dove harp held in the palm of a hand.

Clark holding the
musical bow with
gourd resonator.

One of the more primitive items in the harp collection can best be
described as a "musical bow" with five strings and a half gourd acting
as a resonator attached to a notched stick to separate the strings from
each other. The gourd opening is pressed against the player's chest or
abdomen to increase the sound when plucked.[44]

Another primitive harp in the collection was the Ethiopian harp,
built without use of screws, nail, or glue. The harp was carved out of
wood with a crude hatchet, put together with reeds. Tensioned strings
were attached to the bent twigs. The reeds held the boards, twenty
inches high, fifteen inches wide, and six inches at the soundboard,
together, making a triangular-shaped acoustical cavity. The eight
strings were originally of grass, but the instrument had been restrung

An Ethiopian harp made from wood and twigs.

with catgut. It was said to sound very sweet and melodious in the forest, with considerable power, but inside the sound was diminutive and logy. This instrument was given to Clark by a sailor who obtained it in a village in trade for a jackknife.[45]

An unusual harplike piece in the collection was a tortoise with strings. The myth of Hermes persists in that the tortoise shell gave forth the earliest music when he stepped on it while walking along the Nile. There is an abundance of legendary lore that ascribes the invention of primeval musical instruments to the accidental discovery of pleasing sounds produced by dried sinews stretched tautly across shells of tortoises.[46]

After the death of Melville A. Clark in 1953, Mildred Dilling purchased his famous harp collection.[47] She was a well-known harpist

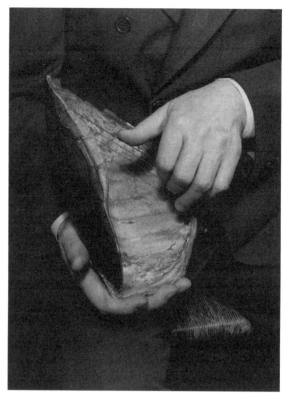

A tortoise shell strung with metal harp strings,
replacing original grass strings.

in New York City who owned the world's largest private collection
of harps. Her collection was donated to Indiana University after her
death on December 30, 1982.[48]

When Clark was asked which collection he favored most, he would
always say, with a twinkle in his eye, the antique harps.[49]

Final Note

IF ONLY I could have met the man! I would love to have sat in Melville Clark's studio while he tuned up his harp, asking him to talk about his life, his interests, and what was on the horizon for his next venture.

Some of my most memorable moments while working on this project were the interviews and informal chats with people who did know him. It was the collective memories and deep feelings of affection expressed by his friends, relatives, customers, fellow musicians, and business associates that kept me from abandoning the work.

Melville Clark preserved an abundance of written material in well-marked folders; had he expected someone one day to chronicle his life's accomplishments? Several generations of harpists owe him a debt of gratitude and appreciation, and my sincerest hope is that, at the very least, these pages will convey his spirit and joie de vivre.

Appendixes

Notes

Selected Bibliography

Index

APPENDIX A

Publications by Melville A. Clark

1910 and 1932. "How to Play the Harp." Harp self-instruction book.

1916–18. Series of twelve articles written for *Crescendo* magazine.

1926. *The Melodeon* [the invention and its manufacture]. Syracuse: Clark Music Company.

1945. "I Played with Wilson." *Christian Science Monitor,* Magazine Section, May 19.

1945. "Music in Industry." *Piano Trade Magazine,* September.

1945. "Let the Lady Speak." *Christian Science Monitor,* Magazine Section, September 15.

1946. "Captured Sound." *Christian Science Monitor,* Magazine Section, December 14.

1947. "Musician Extraordinary." *Opera Concert and Symphony,* March.

1947. "A Hobby Taps Spring to a 'Lost Art.'" *Syracuse Post-Standard,* September 7.

1948. "Music Box for a Princess." *Christian Science Monitor,* Magazine Section, May 22.

1948. "The Rotarian Says It with Music." *Rotarian Magazine,* August.

Serial Numbers and Manufacture Dates for Clark Irish Harps

HARPS WERE SOLD AND RESOLD many times in the Clark Music store as well as in Oliver Ditson's music store in New York City and in the Lyon and Healy (L&H) sales rooms in Chicago and New York. In the process, many sales records containing serial numbers for the Clark Irish Harps were lost. Based on the scanty documentation that remains, here is what we know.

The earliest, prepatent, instruments, forerunners of the standard A models, were made between 1908 and 1910. Clark started numbering the early thirty-one-string harps with number 101 and, according to available records, the smaller twenty-six-string harps with number 01.

The instruments went through several design changes, though the numbering continued. The sequence was interrupted to accommodate the contracts with L&H; new numbering made it easier for L&H to track sales.

The harps that L&H manufactured, starting in 1912, were assigned numbers 300 to 500 for the thirty-one-string A models and numbers 500 to 600 for the twenty-one-string B models. The majority of these harps had the words *Chicago, Illinois* or an L&H brass plate or decal added to their column or both. Some harps even had *Lyon & Healy* hand stenciled onto their columns.

Around 1914, after the patents for the general design of the harp had been granted, a new numbering system for the standard A models, made in Syracuse, was initiated. The serial numbers went from three digits to four, beginning with 1000. L&H continued numbering its productions with three digits, from 300 to 500, as it had been doing since 1912. Then, in 1915, L&H also began to use the four-digit serial numbers, from 1000 to 1999.

Between 1926 and 1948 standard A models made in Syracuse and Chicago were assigned numbers from 2000 to 3000.

The Baby Grand models were made from 1947 to 1953. They were marked "B" or "BG," and their numbering started with B-100. However, many A models that were rebuilt to the specifications of the Baby Grand retained their original serial numbers.

APPENDIX C

Cost of Manufacture of the Clark Irish Harp

SCHEDULE OF OPERATIONS: twenty-two steps in the assembly of a Clark Irish Harp compiled by Melville A. Clark in 1911. Each step has a description of the assembly process, a list of labor and materials, and cost of labor, where appropriate, and materials.

Ideas

Date	
	Subject
	SCHEDULE OF OPERATIONS. CLARKE IRISH HARP.

Operation No.1 — Shaping and fitting top and bottom and back bone for body.

No.2 — Laminating body, Fitting top and body.

" No.3 — Fitting side strips and dound hole strips to body.

" No.4 — Milling maple for front pillar and neck.

" No.5 — Shaping fore pillar, neck and cheek, gluing together pillar neck and cheek.

" No.6 — Gluing and graduating sounding board and fitting both string slips.

" No.7 — Fitting feet and sounding board to body.

" No.8 — Fitting moldings on body and boring pin blocks.

" No.9 — Setting up. (9A Price annalysis wire and gut strings)

" No.10 — Varnishing.

" No.11 — Decorating.

" No.12 — Polishing.

" No.13 — Tuning, pin fitting.

" No.14 — Action Fitting.

" No.15 — Stringing and stretching strings.

" No.16 — Tuning.

" No.17 — Action regulating and tuning.

" No.18 — Tone regulating and inspection.

" No.19 — Oiling off.

" No.20 — Fitting Accessories.

" No.21 — Packing.

" No.22 — Stenciling Box.

Note: Operation No. 6, 7, and 8 combined.
Operation No. 9, 13, 14, 15, 16, 17, 18 combined.
Operation No. 12 and 19 combined.

Ideas

Date

Subject CLARKE IRISH HARP

OPERATION NO. 1

Shaping and fitting top and bottom and back bone for body.

Labor

Shaping, fitting, and trueing top, bottom and back bone, hand and bench work, 2 hr. Schmidt.. $ .62.

Note: Machine sawing bevel on back bone would reduce time required at bench 15 to 30 minutes.

Back Bone pine 7/8

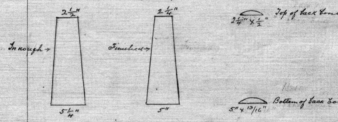

Ends of back bone shaped to a true circle.
Back bone shaped to a true circle.

Material

Bottom chestnut 10 7/8 by 5½ by 7/8 in rough
Top, bottom, and sides sawed on bevel or twist about 5/16
Tone opening 4½ by 1½. Slot 5/16 wide and 5/8 long.

Top chestnut 3½ by 1½ by 7/8 in rough.
Top, bottom and sides sawed on bevel or twist about 3/16.
Top, and bottom blocks hand shaped and finished from the rough.

Same Mfg. Co. 8.68 for 50 sets top and bottom
About 17¢ per pair less mill profit 8¢, Net Cost... $ .09

Back bone, pine....................................... .22
Total................................... .31

Ideas

Date	
	Subject CLARKE IRISH HARP
	OPERATION NO.2

Laminating body, Fitting Top and Bottom.

Labor

Gluing, champing, trimming, shaping, and rough sand papering. Hand and bench work, 3 hrs. Schmidt......$.93

Note: Can not be done by machinery.

Material

Inside veneers plain hard maple.
Outside veneer birdseye maple.
Three or four veneers according to thickness of same.

Grand Rapids Veneer Works, Sept. 1911
    Veneers for 50 harps...........$15.75
    Veneers for one harp............ .32
    Less Mill profit.............. .16..........$.16

𝔌𝔡𝔢𝔞𝔰

𝔇𝔞𝔱𝔢	
	𝔖𝔲𝔟𝔧𝔢𝔠𝔱 CLARKE IRISH HARP
	OPERATION NO. 3

Fitting side strips and sound hole strips to body.

Labor

Fitting side strips and dressing body
hand and bench work, 45 min. Schmidt...............$.24

Note:Can not be done by machinery.

Machine jig sawing sound holes,15 min. Schmidt....$.08

Fitting strips into holes, 1 hr. Schmidt.......... .31

        Total time 2 hours......................$.63

Material

Side strips, spruce 36 inches long 5/16 thick
7/8 wide one end, 5/8 wide other end.
Cut on bevel 1/16 wide at thin edge, cost about...$.02

Sound hole strips bass wood 2 pieces
31 by 3/4 by 1/8,round on one edge.
Cut by workmen sizes required, cost about.........$.02

Ideas

Date

Subject

COST OF MANUFACTURE.

```
Body & work...................$12.50
Bridge Pins...................  .45
Taper Pins....................  1.24
Strings.......................  3.42
Cover.........................  1.50
Key...........................  .50
                              _____
                              $19. 61
```

𝔦𝔡𝔢𝔞𝔰

Date	
	Subject CLARKE IRISH HARP
	OPERATION NO. 4

Milling maple for front pillar and neck..

Labor

Durston Nov. 1911
　　Mill work 50 harps.........$10.50
　　　"　　"　　1 harp.......... .21
　　　　Less Mill profit....... .10................$.11

Material

Otto Nov. 1911
　　50 harps $19.81
　　1　"　...........　.40
　　　　Less Mill profit. .20....................$.20

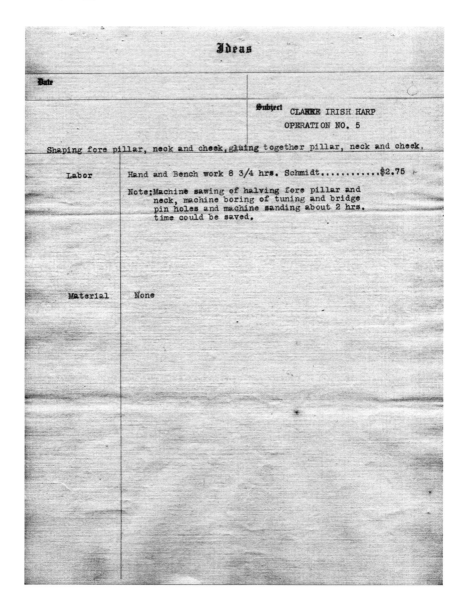

Ideas

Date	
	Subject CLARKE IRISH HARP OPERATION NO. 5

Shaping fore pillar, neck and cheek, gluing together pillar, neck and cheek,

Labor   Hand and Bench work 8 3/4 hrs. Schmidt...........$2.75

Note: Machine sawing of halving fore pillar and
neck, machine boring of tuning and bridge
pin holes and machine sanding about 2 hrs.
time could be saved.

Material   None

𝕴𝖉𝖊𝖆𝖘

Date	
	Subject CLARKE IRISH HARP
	OPERATION NO. 6, 7, & 8

No. 6 Gluing and graduating sounding board and fitting both string slips.
No. 7. Fitting feet and sounding board to body.
No. 8. Fitting moldings on body and boring pin blocks.

Labor Hand and Bench work, 17½ hr (2 days) Schmidt.....$ 7.50

Note: String strips should be made by machinery in
quantity.

Material Sounding board spruce.
Length finished 34 7/8, top 3½, bottom 11 3/4.
Graduated thickness from 1/4 at bottom to 1/16 at top

Sounding boards were bought in the rough at 40¢ each
Less Mill profit.... 20¢.....$.20

String strips and moulding strips hard maple.
Inside string strip 36 long, 1 1/8 wide bottom
5/8 wide at top, 1/4 thick at bottom and 1/8 thick
at top. Cost..................................$.02

Outside string strips, 36 long, by 1/8 thick.
3/4 wide bottom, 7/16 wide at top. Cost............$.02

60 wood screws for fastening sounding board
to body 30 3/4", 30--1/2". Cost.....................$.08
Brads. Cost..$.01
4 wood feet, hard maple. Cost......................$.01
Note: Two feet are 4 long by 1 wide.
Two feet are 3 long by 1 wide.
Total................$.34

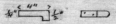

Note: Waste from piano sounding boards can be used
thereby reducing cost.

𝕴𝖉𝖊𝖆𝖘

Date	
	C

Subject CLARKE IRISH HARP

OPERATION NO. 11

Decorating.

Labor

Shamrock, cutting and trimming transfers.
   1½ to 1 3/4 hrs.

Old Irish Art, cutting and trimming transfers
   1½ to 1 3/4 Hrs.

Average time, Warne..............................$.52

Gold leafing for string strips, side molding
and tone holes.
1st process, sizing
2nd process, applying and trimming leaf.
3rd process, laquering.
2 hrs. Revoir...................................$.68

Material

Shamrock, transfers complete......................$1.44
Old Irish Art, transfers complete................ 1.05

Gold Leaf, one book............................... .40
Size and laquer................................... .05

Shamrock transfers, gold leaf, size and laquer.... 1.89   +

Note: Dutch metal could be used instead of gold leaf,
      or natural finish mahogany strips reducing cost.

Ideas

Date	
	Subject CLARKE IRISH HARP
	OPERATION 12, & 19.
	Polishing and oiling off.

Labor

Rubbing **twice over** with pumice stone and rotten stone.
Hand polishing with rotten stone and oiling off.
3 to 5 hrs. according to conditon of harp.
Average four hours, Warne.................$1.28

Material

Pumice stone, rotton stone......................$.05

𝕴𝖉𝖊𝖆𝖘

𝕭𝖆𝖙𝖊	

𝕾𝖚𝖇𝖏𝖊𝖈𝖙 CLARKE IRISH HARP
OPERATION NO. 9, 13, 14,
15, 16, 17, 18.

Setting Up.

Labor

Reaming out tuning pin holes and fitting pins.
" " bridge pin holes and fitting pins
Guaging and putting in finger sharpening holes,
tapping for thread, and fitting sharps.
Cleaning our string pin holes on strip slip.
Fitting pegs into pin holes to hold string.
Putting on feet and bolt, fitting and adjusting brass
collar, brass plate on botton of post, name plate on
bottom of body, and felt pads on batton of feet.
Stringing and stretching all strings, tuning, action
and tone regulating. 10 hrs., Revoir..................$3.40

Note: Time can be reduced two hours in a well
organized factory when harps are set up in quantities.

Material

30 string pins @ 2¢ each............$.60
30 bridge pins @ 1½¢ each........... .45
30 tuning pins @ 3 1/3¢ each........1.00
30 tone sharpeners @ 2½¢ each........ .75
1 brass collar and 1 brass plate.... .02
1 plate "Patents Pending".......... .02
4 felt pads........................ .01
1 iron bolt and washer............. .01
5 base wire strings................ .35
25 gut strings.....................1.85
1 plate on botton of harp,
   Signature and number........... .04
                              ───────
                              Total $5.10

Note: Price of strings can be greatly reduced by being
specially made in Germany or France, in coils.

Note: Leaving off bridge pins would reduce labor one half
hour, 17¢, and cost of pins, 45¢, total 62¢

Note: Price on tone sharpeners are quotations from
Cortland Carriage Goods Co., Dec. 2, 1911, 1 to
5 thousand lots, not including cost of dies.

Note: Price on tuning pins from bill Hartford Machine
Screw Co., Nov. 21, 1911 as part of 4,000 lot.
In lots of 10,000 price would probably be reduced
20 to 30%

Ideas

Date	
	Subject CLARKE IRISH HARP OPERATION NO. 10.

Varnishing.

Labor

Shellacing one coat complete 10 min.
         two   "   " 20 "
        Three "   " 30 "

Varnishing one coat complete 20 min.
        Two "   " 40 "
        Three"   " 60 "

Note:Number of coats required is according to
    condition of the wood work and temperature.

Three coats shellac and three coats of varnish
1½ hrs. Wern...$.51

Material

Body, shellac one coat or more.
Body, varnish, two or three coats.

Sounding board, shellac two coats
    "   " , varnish two coats.

Neck and arm, shellac one coat
   "   "   " , varnish two or three coats.

Shellac for all, one half pint.........................$.22
Varnish for all one pint.............................. .38
        Total................................$.60

Ideas

Date	
	Subject CLARKE IRISH HARP
	OPERATION NO.21

Packing.

Labor   Making packing box, fastening harp in box
with excelsior pad and brace, 1 hr.10 min........$.27

Material   Lumber...$.65
Excelsior 2½ pounds................................ .05
Paper... .03
Nails ½ pound..................................... .03
                           Total.................... .76

LH paid 50 per crate lumber

Ideas

Date	
	Subject CLARKE IRISH HARP
	OPERATION NO. 22
	Stenciling. or marking box.
Labor	$.05
Material	$.03

Ideas

Date	
	Dec. 12/11
	Subject
	LAMINATING NECK--TWO PIECES.

For

Extra strength obtained.

Against

With natural wood finish a dark streak would show, where parts are laminated, resembling a crack in the wood. This streak would not show on finish other than natural wood.

More and thicker lumber would be required, as the rough lumber should be $1\frac{1}{2}$ inches thick, straight and true and free from warp.

The two pieces must be dressed on four sides, as against two dressing on one piece and must be dressed down from $2\frac{1}{2}$ inches in the rough to about $1\frac{1}{2}$ inches finished.

Additional labor required would be about $\frac{1}{2}$ hour, cost 16¢.

Increase in cost of lumber required would be about 10¢ per harp.

Ideas

Date	
	Subject
	TENATIVE PROPOSITION ON MANUFACTURE OF CLARKE IRISH HARP (CONTINUED)

70 sheets Clark Irish Harp, Syracuse, N.Y.
  5 sets per sheet, 5¢ per sheets.........$350

                                 $247.26

Gold Leafing neck and post
  Additonal cost.
    Labor $2.38
    Mat'l   1.00

            $3.38

Ideas

Unit

1000 harps per year : 3½ per day

~~Date~~

Gold Harp — Junior Harp

Subject

COST OF MANUFACTURE.

1000 cases
10,000 cases.

21²² doz

Kahki cases...................	$1.75
Wood work..................	13.50
Finishing...................	3.00
machine parts..............	2.07
Pegs.......................	.60
Strings....................	3.00
Assembling.................	2.00
Key........................	.50
Box........................	.60
Cover......................	.25
High-Low Base..............	

Notes

Abbreviations

The following abbreviations have been used in the notes in citing source material locations:

LPK-C   Linda Pembroke Kaiser's Collection
OHA   Onondaga Historical Association
SUL   Syracuse University Library, Special Collections Research Center

Many of the Clark and Syracuse Symphony Orchestra (SSO) materials are duplicated in several places. Citations in the selected bibliography refer to the location at which the resource material was initially noted by the author.

1. Melville Clark: The Man and His Family

1. Uncle Melville Clark took out more than two hundred patents in his lifetime. Most of them are on the player piano, particularly on the transposing device and the recording mechanism for reproducing the player's exact interpretation of the composition.

2. Melville A. Clark, *Crescendo* (1923), 1, LPK-C.

3. "Clark Music Firm Dates Back to 1858," *Syracuse Post-Standard,* 1935 clipping, LPK-C.

4. "Former Syracusan a Noted Inventor," *Syracuse Herald,* June 30, 1912. Uncle Melville Clark became a clarinetist and martial fife player in the Union army and was present when General Lee surrendered.

5. Nevart Apikian, "Musicians at Home," *Syracuse Post-Standard,* October 23, 1949.

6. Clark family event log, 1841–1932, LPK-C.

7. Clark autobiographical statement 6, LPK-C. The author has many such statements by Clark, ranging from one to sixteen pages.

8. Clark, "How the Clark Irish Harp Came About" (public lecture, n.d.), LPK-C.

9. Clark autobiographical statement 6, LPK-C.

10. Clark autobiographical statement 3, LPK-C.

11. Clark, "Music: My Hobby, My Profession, and Business" (public lecture, 1948), 13, LPK-C.

12. Twelfth Annual National Harp Festival program, April 16–17, 1932, LPK-C.

13. "Clark Music Firm Dates Back to 1859 in City," *Syracuse Journal,* August 3, 1919.

14. The Clarks also purchased the Memory Farm and Upper Drovers' Farm on Palmer Road in Oran, New York, a total of 425 acres.

15. Apikian, "Musicians at Home."

16. Clark to Trudy Feliu, Music Department, *Life,* June 8, 1950.

17. The present owners of Drovers' Tavern are Lance and Susan McKee.

18. Frances Magnum, "Musician Also a Farmer—and a Success at Both," *Washington Post,* May 23, 1935.

19. Anabel Parker McCann, "From Piano to Plowing," *New York Sun,* March 11, 1936.

20. Melville Clark Jr., conversation with author, June 9, 2008.

21. Though Melville Jr., Dorothy, and Timothy did not become professional performers, they had been trained to play several instruments and were all gifted musicians. Melville Jr. became a research engineer in the field of sound. Dorothy worked in public administration, and Timothy became a successful real estate broker.

22. *Melville Clark, Harpist, and Dorothy Clark at the Novachord* (concert program, March 27, 1939, Hotel Somerset, Boston), LPK-C.

23. Clark studied cello with Paul Ludwig and Ernest Mather in Syracuse and with Joseph Hollman and Hugo Becker in London.

24. Grace Follet, "Melville Clark," *Harp News,* Spring 1954, 10–11, LPK-C.

25. "Clark Never Travels Without Beloved Harp," *Syracuse Journal,* December 30, 1935.

26. Nevart Apikian to author, Syracuse, October 2, 2006.

27. At the time of Clark's death he was developing a fiberglass harp; finishing a compendium on the harp history of the world, *Singing Strings;* and assembling the recently purchased Wurlitzer pedal-harp components. Invitations had been sent to friends and patrons for a gala commemorating the hundredth year of the Steinway piano.

28. E. J. B., "Striking Tribute Paid at Funeral," *Syracuse Post-Standard,* December 15, 1953, LPK-C.

2. The House That Clark Built

1. Joseph Adams, "History of Music Reflected in Collection by Syracusan," *Syracuse Post-Standard,* October 25, 1939.

2. Clark autobiographical statement 2, LPK-C.

3. Clark, "George W. Clark Enters Business," March 18, 1932, Family Biography folder, LPK-C.

4. Clark to E. Cowe, September 26, 1849, SUL.

5. Clark, "Music: My Hobby," 3 (see chap. 1, n. 11).

6. Subsequently, Melville Clark went to Grand Haven, Michigan, and started a second manufacturing company, the Melville Clark Company. It enabled him to develop the player-piano mechanism independently. He eventually returned to Chicago.

7. "Piano Recording Mechanism," *Musical Age,* February 14, 1911, 58, LPK-C.

8. Clark, "Music: My Hobby," 4.

9. Ibid., 5.

10. Clark, "George Clark and His Family," March 18, 1932, 1, LPK-C.

11. Ibid.

12. George Clark to Clark, November 9, 1905, LPK-C.

13. Clark Music Company statistics, 1841–1932, LPK-C.

14. Arthur Clark to Clark Music directors and officers, November 15, 1909, LPK-C.

15. Clark to Adelaide Emmerich, August 1, 1911, SUL.

16. Clark Music Company statistics, 1841–1932, LPK-C.

17. "Clark Music Firm Dates to 1858 in City," *Syracuse Post-Standard,* April 6, 1949.

18. Clark to Benjamin H. Jefferson, January 6, 1920, LPK-C.

19. "Present Head Outstanding Figure in Music Life of Nation," *Syracuse Post-Standard,* April 6, 1949.

20. Clark, "Music: My Hobby," 15.

21. W. Judd (Clark sales manager) to Syracuse Art Club, 1922, Clark Music Company folder, LPK-C.

22. Clark, "The History of the Syracuse Symphony Orchestra" (lecture, 1925), SUL.

23. "In Grateful Appreciation," *Syracuse Post-Standard,* July 30, 1953.

24. "Syracuse Sponsor 16 Years on Air Without a Break," *Broadcasting,* July 15, 1938, 24, LPK-C.

25. "Syracusans See First Local Video Program," *Syracuse Herald-Journal,* December 2, 1948.

26. *Successful School Band* (Clark Music Company brochure), 1929, LPK-C.

27. Melville Clark Jr., conversation with author, June 18, 2005.

28. Marion Sinclair, harpist, conversation with author, May 4, 1992.

29. Barbara Lang Buckland, harpist, conversation with author, May 31, 2006.

30. P. D. Fahnstock, "Sound Merchandising Practices," *Music Trade Review,* August 1929, 8, SUL.

31. Clark appeared three times in Ripley's "Believe It or Not" column in the *Syracuse Journal*. The December 31, 1932, column showed unusual potted palms displayed in the Clark Music Company store that needed to be fed a quart of oysters twice a year; the April 17, 1934, column pictured Clark playing two harps at one time; and the March 6, 1947, column pictured Clark with the world's smallest perfect violin, 1/64th size.

32. Clark, "Who Will Carry On?" autobiographical statement 13, 5, LPK-C.

33. Clark to Carlos Salzedo, July 24, 1946, LPK-C.

34. Clark to William Place, September 19, 1950, LPK-C.

35. Clark to John F. Wild, October 7, 1950, SUL.

36. Robert Sharp, Clark piano technician, conversations with author, June 20, 2005, and June 10, 2008.

37. Melville Clark Jr. recalls that harp manufacturing was also discontinued for financial reasons. After the sale of materials, Hildebrandt indeed did make harps out of his home for a while.

38. Contract between Clark Music Company and Eric Hildebrandt, June 9, 1954, LPK-C.

39. Kenneth Williams, Clark piano technician, conversation with author, June 18, 2005.

40. Frank De Fonda, Clark sales manager, conversation with author, June 17, 2005.

3. The Clark Irish Harp

1. Clark, "Music: My Hobby," 9 (see chap. 1, n. 11).

2. Clark, "The Clark Irish Harp" (public lecture, 1946), 1, LPK-C.

3. Exact dates of his educational experiences are unavailable.

4. Clark to A. Gainey, October 21, 1908, SUL.

5. Clark, "Music: My Hobby," 9.

6. Ibid.

7. Ibid., 10.

8. Clark, "How I Came to Invent the Clark Irish Harp," 1942, 20, Clark Irish Harp folder, LPK-C.

9. Ibid., 2.

10. Ibid.

11. Clark, "The Irish Harp" (transcript from lecture material), LPK-C.

12. Roslyn Rensch, *Harps and Harpists*, 2nd ed. (Bloomington: Indiana Univ. Press, 2007), 120.

13. Clark, "How I Came to Invent the Clark Irish Harp," 2.

14. *Hall O'Harps Monthly* 12 (December 1919): 2, LPK-C.

15. Clark Harp Manufacturing Company, *Clark Irish Harp* (promotional pamphlet, n.d.), 15, LPK-C.

16. Ibid., 23.

17. Joan Clark, "Melville Clark and the Clark Irish Harp," *Folk Harp Journal* 96 (1997): 55.

18. Clark Harp Manufacturing Company, *Clark Irish Harp,* 24.

19. The twenty-eight plates were engraved by the John Worley Company, Music Printers and Engravers, Stanhope Street, Boston, August 12, 1910, SUL.

20. *Who's Who in America,* 1920.

21. Clark to Mrs. George Briggs, September 8, 1909, SUL.

22. Clark to Emmerich, August 1, 1911, SUL.

23. Program for lecture concert, Lincoln Hall, March 18, 1910, LPK-C.

24. Clark to John Finlay, March 10, 1910, SUL.

25. Clark to Mrs. Christopher Marks, October 1, 1911, SUL.

26. Clark to (Uncle Melville) Clark, April 4, 1912, SUL.

27. Clark to J. Allen (of the *Christian Science Monitor*), June 8, 1912, SUL.

28. Contract between Lyon and Healy, Chicago, and Clark Harp Manufacturing Company, March 21, 1912, SUL.

29. Clark to Van Veachton Rogers, July 3, 1916, SUL.

30. Clark Manufacturing Company to J. C. Freeman, Lyon and Healy, December 13, 1916, SUL.

31. R. Keenly to Clark, October 4, 1935, SUL.

32. Clark to Rogers, July 3, 1916, SUL.

33. Rogers to Clark, December 28, 1912, SUL.

34. Clark to Rogers, September 9, 1912, SUL.

35. Rogers to Clark, letters 1913–14, SUL.

36. Red Path Chautauqua Circuit itineraries, 1913–14, SUL.

37. Clark to William Flint, January 19, 1910, SUL.

38. J. Russell Paine to Rogers, April 28, 1914, SUL.

39. Clark Harp Manufacturing Company, *Clark Irish Harp,* 20.

40. Clark to Leah Haywood, November 1, 1912, SUL.

41. *Hall O'Harps Monthly* 1–3 (n.d.), LPK-C.

42. A. Francis Pinto, "The Possibility of the Clark Irish Harp," *Crescendo,* 1916, LPK-C.

43. Irish Harps Sold folder, Clark Papers, LPK-C.

44. Actions-Improvements folder, Clark Papers, LPK-C.

45. Clark, "Specifications for Style 'D,'" *Clark Irish Harp,* November 1, 1919, LPK-C.

46. Clark to Zoe Cheskin, June 5, 1931, SUL.

47. Clark Patent no. 1,351,468, March 31, 1920, Arsalaan Fay Collection, Sarasota, Florida.

48. Ibid.

49. Clark Music Company harp brochure, SUL.

50. Clark to Rembert Wurlitzer, September 23, 1952, LPK-C.

51. According to Clark's notes and sketches, the fiberglass harp had these dimensions and specifications: 30-inch length of shell, 4¾-inch depth of bottom, 8-inch width at bottom, 3⅜-inch width at top, 1¾-inch depth at top, E as the lowest string, harp equipped with movable feet to enable harp to rest on player's knees, and no bridge pins.

52. Clark to Victor Todd, Lunn Laminates, October 30, 1953, LPK-C.

53. Clark, "Melodies in Plastic and Nylon," *Modern Plastics,* November 1951, SUL.

54. Rees Harpsicles are brightly colored small, portable harps manufactured since 2003 by the William Rees Company in Rising Sun, Indiana.

55. Clark, Concert Programs folder, LPK-C.

56. H. Louden to Clark, March 1926, SUL.

57. Antarctic Expedition folder, Clark Papers, LPK-C.

58. Robert K. Headland, *Chronological List of Antarctic Expeditions and Related Historical Events* (Cambridge: Cambridge Univ. Press, 1990).

59. Ibid.

60. Ibid.

61. C. E. Rofgren to Clark, February 1, 1929, LPK-C.

62. Dr. Dana Coman to Clark, February 1929, LPK-C.

63. Ibid.

64. Adm. Richard E. Byrd to Clark, citation, Byrd Aviation Associates, 1930, LPK-C.

65. Clark to Fitzsimmons, August 11, 1908, SUL.

66. Clark, "Comparison of the Clark Irish Harp as Found and as Perfected," April 23, 1912, Actions-Improvements folder, Clark Papers, LPK-C.

4. Birth of the Nylon Harp String

1. "Birth of the Nylon Harp String," *International Folk Harp Journal* 114 (2001): 43–44.

2. Alice F. Keegan, "Musical History Recorded as Clark Plays Harp with New Nylon Strings," *Syracuse Post-Standard,* February 13, 1948, LPK-C.

3. Dewey Owens, *From Aeolian to Thunder* (Chicago: Lyon and Healy Harps, 1992), 110.

4. J. George Morley, *Strings, Stringing, and Tuning* (London: A. R. Sidders, 1918), 9, LPK-C.

5. Clark, "How the Clark Nylon Harp String Came About" (lecture, 1948), 9, LPK-C.

6. Clark to R. H. Carter, E. I. du Pont Nylon Sales, June 20, 1948.

7. Clark, "Plastics in the Art of Music" (lecture, 1948), 3, LPK-C.

8. "Plastics in Harp Provide Tone Insurance," *Modern Plastics,* November 1951.

9. Du Pont to Clark, October 16, 1947, LPK-C.

10. Ibid.

11. Clark to du Pont (last letter), August 20, 1953, LPK-C.

12. Keegan, "Musical History Recorded."

13. "Strings for Harps Are Made of Nylon," *New York Times,* January 21, 1948.

14. "Harp under Water," *Life,* December 13, 1948, 80.

15. Keegan, "Musical History Recorded."

16. Morley, *Strings, Stringing, and Tuning,* 9.

17. "Strings for Harps."

5. Inventions and Ideas

1. "Syracuse Man Invents Clever Fruit Picker," *Syracuse Post-Standard,* July 16, 1917, LPK-C.

2. Clark, "'No Bruise' Fruit Picker," LPK-C.

3. Ibid.

4. Clark, Patents and Drawings folder, LPK-C.

5. C. E. Kilbourne to Clark, numerous letters, 1913–17, LPK-C.

6. Clark to H. R. Gillette, August 20, 1917, LPK-C.

7. "Syracusans Sell Invention to Aid Change of Records," *Syracuse Post-Standard,* September 8, 1929, LPK-C.

8. Virgil Clymer was a partner in the law firm of Nottingham, Clymer, Smith, and Paltz. He was chairman of the Board of Supervisors of Onondaga County and a member of the Onondaga County Draft Board in World War I.

9. *Davy Automatic Fire Escape* (brochure), LPK-C.

10. C. S. Joyce, secretary of the Senate Technical Committee of the Committee on Commerce, U.S. Senate, to Clark, March 3, 1936, LPK-C.

11. "Syracuse Men Developing Safety Device for Sea Use," *Syracuse Post-Standard,* June 30, 1935, LPK-C.

12. "Complete Protection Auto Bumper," blueprint, June 1, 1927, LPK-C.

13. Auto Guard folder, LPK-C.

14. Clark to Charles Franklin Kettering, September 1, 1936, SUL. Kettering invented the first electrical ignition system for the self-starter for automobile engines in 1915.

15. Personal Letters folder, LPK-C.

16. Patent Pending no. 198-413, issued June 13, 1927, LPK-C.

17. Patent no. 1,896,683, issued February 7, 1933, LPK-C.

18. "Device Builds Tonal Balance," *Christian Science Monitor*, November 23, 1932, LPK-C; "Device Opens New Music Era," *Syracuse Journal*, January 14, 1932, LPK-C.

19. Ibid.

20. "Melville Clark Wins Praise of Stokowski," *Syracuse Sunday American*, January 17, 1932, LPK-C.

21. Dr. Melville Clark Jr., conversation with author, January 16, 2003.

22. Clark, Inventions and Patents folder, 1925–35, LPK-C.

23. Ibid.

24. Clark, "Visualite, a New Mysterious Plastic" (lecture, 1947), LPK-C.

25. Clark, Inventions and Patents folder, LPK-C.

26. Clark, "Let the Lady Speak," *Christian Science Monitor*, September 15, 1945.

6. The First Syracuse Symphony Orchestra

1. In 1921, when only sixty-five U.S. cities had populations above 100,000, the population of Syracuse was 171,000.

2. Clark, "History of the SSO," 1925, SUL. From its inception the first SSO enjoyed great cooperation and valuable connections with Syracuse University. De Pavaloff, visiting violinist at SU, selected and rehearsed the very first orchestra players. Dr. Berwald was engaged to be the second conductor and music director. Mrs. Winfield Chapin, chairman of the Patrons Committee, made gifts of concert tickets to SU students in the College of Fine Arts. Later, during the fourth season, she funded five Symphony Scholarships for SU music students. To further strengthen the ties, the third conductor, Vladimir Shavitch, taught ten-week conducting classes at SU, and his wife, Tina Lerner, presented two master classes in piano studies both semesters. Dr. Polah was concertmaster in the later days of the SSO under Shavitch and later became conductor of the reorganized WPA-supported Syracuse Federal Symphony.

3. "How the Syracuse Orchestra Was Born," *Women's Home Companion*, June 1921, LPK-C.

4. The Clark Music Building was located at 416 South Salina Street; the old Grand Opera House stood at the corner of Clinton and Washington streets.

5. According to an undated clipping from the Onondaga Historical Association, Berwald studied at Stuttgart Music Conservatory in Germany. He became the conductor of the orchestra and choral society in Liebau, Russia. After he immigrated to the United States he was hired in 1892 to become a professor of piano, music history, and theory, as well as music director, at Syracuse University. As a composer he published more than four hundred works.

6. Clark, "The History of the SSO" (lecture, 1925), SUL.

7. B. F. Keith's vaudeville theater opened on January 26, 1920. It stood at 412 South Salina Street.

8. Philip Daly, "Looking Back," *Syracuse Post-Standard,* December 29, 1953, LPK-C. "It was a promotional project for Keith's Theatre. It was a way to get customers into the new auditorium and maybe watch a movie after the concert."

9. "Symphony Is Formed Here by Musicians," *Syracuse Journal,* November 11, 1921, SUL.

10. Original SSO Board of Officers, 1921 (LPK-C): Melville Clark, president; Aurin Chase, vice president; George F. Wilson, secretary; Ralph B. Palmatier, assistant secretary; Glenn L. Chesbro, treasurer; Andrew Goettel, librarian; Alexander G. Strong; Myron Levee; and Rudolph Miller.

11. Clark to Syracuse Chamber of Commerce, February 2, 1922, SUL.

12. Clark to Victor Herbert, April 7, 1922, SUL; Clark to *Music Trade Indicator,* January 17, 1922, SUL.

13. Executive board to SSO players, January 24, 1922, SUL.

14. SSO stationery, 1921–22, LPK-C.

15. Clark to Chamber of Commerce, LPK-C.

16. SSO board minutes, June 1923, LPK-C.

17. Clark to Professor Shea, March 23, 1922, SUL. Following is the children's assembly plan:

TABLE 2. Children's assembly plan

School	Teacher	No. of children	Meeting place
Onondaga Valley	Miss Spencer	150	Dey Bros.
House of Providence	Sister Marie	150	Larkins
Bellevue		200	Burns Shoes
McKinley		200	Empire Theatre
Onondaga Orphans Home	Mr. McHugh	130	Corner of Jefferson and Salina
Danforth		200	O'Malley's Women's Shop
Holy Rosary		200	Bessie-Sprague's
Lincoln		300	Clark Music Company
Grant		200	Wm. Peck's Millinery
Edward Smith		200	Palmer-Reeve
Franklin		200	Nye's Drug Store
Assumption Academy	Mr. Ethan	40	Carlton Shop

18. Clark to Anna Morrison, March 23, 1922, LPK-C.

19. "How the SSO Was Born," LPK-C.

20. SSO publicity brochure, 1922, LPK-C.

21. Clark note to SSO Board, 1922, SUL.

22. SSO Board minutes, SUL.

23. Clark, "Story of the SSO," 1925, SUL.

24. Clark to Charlton Loudon, Carnegie Hall booking agent, October 10, 1923, SUL.

25. "Rave Reviews," *Syracuse Journal,* March 30, 1924.

26. Clark to Mrs. H. W. Chapin, October 11, 1924, SUL.

27. Sharpe to Shavitch, July 8, 1924, SUL.

28. European conductors: Wilhelm Furtwängler, New York Philharmonic; Otto Klemperer, New York Symphony; and Serge Koussevitsky, Boston Symphony Orchestra, LPK-C.

29. Shavitch articles, *Syracuse Telegram* and *Syracuse Journal,* March 1924.

30. Clark to John McCormack, August 26, 1924, SUL.

31. Clark to Herbert, July 1924, SUL.

32. Herbert to Clark, July 1924, SUL.

33. "Symphony to Get Victor Herbert Library of Music," *Syracuse Journal,* November 8, 1924.

34. "Symphony Orchestra to Be Incorporated," *Syracuse Journal,* September 30, 1925.

35. Martin Knapp (1881–1959) was a local attorney who practiced with Nottingham and Nottingham. He was the husband of Sally Hazard, whose grandfather Frederick R. Hazard founded Solvay Process.

36. Clark, "History of the Syracuse Symphony," 1925, SUL.

37. Edward F. Albee to SSO executive board, October 1, 1924, SUL.

38. Louis Crabtree, "Aid the Symphony Orchestra," *Syracuse Sunday American,* March 2, 1925.

39. Melville A. Clark, Secretary, Minutes of the Central New York Music Festival, 1923–25, LPK-C.

40. Fifth Season SSO Concert Programs, 1925–26, LPK-C.

41. "Concerts for Students at Central High," *Syracuse Journal,* October 2, 1925.

42. "Seek $30,000 to Meet Debt of Symphony," *Syracuse Journal,* January 31, 1926.

43. Louis Crabtree, "Auditorium Seating 5,000 Urgently Needed," *Syracuse Sunday American,* February 8, 1926.

44. The Strand Theatre stood on the corner of Salina and Harrison streets.

45. SSO Concert Programs, LPK-C.

46. Emma Van Wormer, "Talking It Over," *Syracuse Herald-Journal*, February 18, 1958.

47. Robert W. Friedel, "Prokofieff Pleases," *Syracuse Journal*, February 28, 1926.

48. "Carrying Music to North," *Syracuse Journal*, October 27, 1926.

49. "SSO Ends with Deficit," *Syracuse Journal*, March 14, 1928.

50. "Shavitch Granted Leave to Lead Berlin Orchestra," *Syracuse Post-Standard*, February 12, 1929.

51. "Central Figures in Music Dispute," *Syracuse Journal*, August 29, 1932.

52. "Symphony Concerts to Be Continued," *Syracuse Journal*, August 30, 1932.

53. Martha Wheatly, "Grainger Plays Brahms," *Syracuse Herald*, February 19, 1933.

54. "Shavitch to Russia," *Syracuse Journal*, May 14, 1933.

55. "Symphony Concerts to Be Continued," *Syracuse Journal*, May 14, 1933.

56. *New Grove Dictionary of American Music* (New York: Macmillan, 1986), 4:341.

57. "Victor Miller Made Head of Symphony," *Syracuse Herald-Journal*, October 10, 1933.

58. "Talking It Over," *Syracuse Herald-Journal*, October 10, 1933.

59. "Concerts to Be Free," *Syracuse Herald-Journal*, March 12, 1934.

60. Ibid.

61. "Muench to Pick," *Syracuse Herald-Journal*, March 12, 1934.

62. "The Concert," *Syracuse Herald-Journal*, December 1, 1939.

63. "Syracuse Orchestra Is Completely Reorganized," *Syracuse Herald-Journal*, January 30, 1940.

64. "The People's Symphony" (program notes of the Syracuse Philharmonic Orchestra), February 25, 1951, LPK-C.

65. Murray Bernthal, conversation with author, February 1, 2003.

66. The Syracuse Civic Music Association and Morning Musicals also merged in 1950 to become Civic Morning Musicals, Inc.

67. Susan W. Larson, "Syracuse Symphony Orchestras 1848–1969," June 30, 1970, OHA.

7. Singing Troops and War Balloons

1. "City Played Host to Wartime Camp," *Syracuse Journal*, March 20, 1939, OHA.

2. Harry Barnhart was famous for being the leader of the Community Chorus of New York City. His name appears in the Song and Light Festival souvenir program, U.S.A. Mobilization Camp, August 9, 1917, LPK-C.

3. Clark and Margaret Wilson had collaborated on several professional musical programs before World War I.

4. Clark to Lester Markel, editor, *New York Times Magazine,* June 17, 1942, LPK-C.

5. "Deadly Balloon Offensive," *Piano Trades* (Chicago), February 19, 1918, SUL.

6. Clark's uncle was the inventor of the Apollo player piano and a partner in the Story and Clark Piano Company.

7. (Uncle Melville) Clark to Clark, August 29, 1917, SUL.

8. Clark to (Uncle Melville) Clark, September 5, 1917, SUL.

9. Clark to R. Ross, September 4, 1917, SUL.

10. Ibid.

11. "Carries Truth to Germans," *Syracuse Post-Standard,* May 5, 1919, SUL.

12. "Enemy Morale Shattered by Syracuse Man's Genius," *Syracuse Post-Standard,* April 28, 1919, SUL.

13. Clark to (Uncle Melville) Clark, August 29, 1917, SUL.

14. Clark to National Weather Bureau, Washington, D.C., August 27, 1917, SUL.

15. Clark to Howe-Bauman, September 27, 1917, SUL; Clark to Goodyear Rubber Company, September 7, 1917, SUL.

16. Clark to Miller Rubber Company, September 5, 1917, SUL.

17. "Endorsed by Northcliffe," *Syracuse Post-Standard,* August 20, 1917, SUL.

18. Chemist John D. Pennock of Solvay Process in Solvay, New York, conducted the experiments.

19. "Paper Balloon Goes 600 Miles," *Syracuse Post-Standard,* August 31, 1917, SUL.

20. "War Balloon Planned by M. A. Clark," *Syracuse Post-Standard,* April 4, 1919, SUL.

21. "Endorsed by Northcliffe."

22. Bert Ford, "British Propaganda Campaign in Germany a Complete Success," *Syracuse Post-Standard,* September 10, 1919, SUL.

23. Ibid.

8. White House Connections

1. Clark, "President Wilson," Wilson folder, LPK-C.

2. Clark, "Melville Clark at White House," *Music Trade Review,* September 1914, LPK-C.

3. "Receives White House Gift," *Syracuse Post-Standard,* June 5, 1914.

4. Clark, "I Played the Harp for Wilson," *Christian Science Monitor,* May 19, 1945.

5. George Donaldson, "Margaret Wilson Made Her Debut Here in 1915," *Syracuse Herald-American,* March 30, 1947, LPK-C.

6. A. Walter Kramer, "Roosevelt and Margaret Wilson in Huge Audience at Syracuse Festival," *Musical America,* May 15, 1915, LPK-C.

7. "Roosevelt-Barnes Trial on Tomorrow," special to *New York Times,* April 17, 1915.

8. Wilson to Clark correspondence, 1914–24, SUL.

9. "Diplomatic Dinner," *Washington Times,* January 26, 1916, clipping, LPK-C.

10. "Miss Wilson to Sing at Camps," *Brooklyn Citizen,* March 13, 1918, SUL.

11. Wilson to Clark, July 16, 1923, SUL.

12. Henry Junge to Clark, April 30, 1935, SUL.

13. "Melville Clark's Harp Wins Admiration of Pres. Roosevelt at the White House Dinner," *Syracuse Herald,* May 20, 1935, SUL.

14. Presidential Inaugural Invitation packet, January 20, 1937, SUL.

9. The Collections

1. According to a letter from Harry Clifton, Clark hired him in 1947 at thirty-three cents an hour to assist with the sorting and organizing of the collected specimens, while he was recuperating in the Onondaga Sanatorium.

2. Clark, "I Also Collect Stamps" (article for stamp collectors' lecture, October 10, 1946), LPK-C.

3. "Clark to Show Early Victor Phonograph at Music Fair," *Syracuse Post-Standard,* July 4, 1948, LPK-C.

4. Susan T. Stinson, Belfer Audio Laboratory and Archive.

5. A saltbox house is a distinctive open-air shed used for the solar evaporation process in the production of salt. The last solar salt yard closed in 1926.

6. *Christian Science Monitor,* Magazine Section, May 22, 1948, LPK-C.

7. "Music Boxes Displayed for Christmas," *Syracuse Post-Standard,* March 18, 1948, LPK-C.

8. Clark, "A Hobby Taps Spring to a 'Lost Art,'" *Syracuse Post-Standard,* September 7, 1947, LPK-C.

9. Clark, "Music Box for a Princess," *Retail Merchant Magazine,* August 8, 1948, 4, LPK-C.

10. *Arizona Republic* (Phoenix), April 17, 1948, LPK-C.

11. Clark to John Colville, February 2, 1948, LPK-C.

12. Colville to Clark, March 16, 1948, SUL.

13. Clark handwritten notes, April 1948, LPK-C.

14. Publication release to Syracuse newspapers, for April 11, 1948, LPK-C.

15. Clark to Arthur H. Wyman, RCA Victor Division, May 6, 1948, LPK-C.

16. Clark, "Music Box for a Princess," *Christian Science Monitor,* Magazine Section, May 22, 1948, LPK-C.

17. Bill Leonard, "This Is New York with Bill Leonard Reporting," WCBS Radio, April 13, 1948, LPK-C.

18. "Cloud Chorus, Led by Clark on Plane Trip," *Syracuse Post-Standard,* July 3, 1948, LPK-C.

19. *Bulletin and Scots Pictorial* (Glasgow), April 21, 1948, 4, LPK-C.

20. Nevart Apikian, "Music Box Delighted Princess," *Syracuse Post-Standard,* April 28, 1948, LPK-C.

21. Clark, "Music Box," 4.

22. Clark, "A Date with Royalty" (notes for a lecture, 1948), LPK-C.

23. Ibid.

24. Ibid.; Clark lecture notes, Music Box folder, LPK-C.

25. Apikian, "Music Box Delighted Princess."

26. "Syracusans See Initial Telecast," December 1, 1948, *Syracuse Herald-Journal,* Herald-Journal files, Onondaga County Public Library.

27. Thola T. Schenck, "Where There Was Truly Music in the Air," *Syracuse Post-Standard,* Sunday News, December 1944, LPK-C.

28. Donald House, interview by author, July 17, 2006, Syracuse.

29. Clark lecture to the Pictures Club, *Syracuse Post-Standard,* February 25, 1946, SUL.

30. Clark to Charles Hardy, Jamesville, Wisconsin, October 19, 1950, SUL.

31. The seraphin(e) is a wind instrument whose sounding parts are reeds, consisting of thin tongues of brass that vibrate freely through a slot in a plate. It has a fixed case like a pianoforte.

32. Clark, "List of Antique Instruments," 1949, SUL.

33. "Indian Plays Harmonium," *Syracuse Post-Standard,* May 1947, OHA.

34. Clark, "List of Antique Instruments."

35. Melville Clark Collection of Rare Musical Instruments, list from Clark materials, LPK-C.

36. Clark, "Henry Ford: An Impression" (lecture, April 1947), 1, LPK-C.

37. Ibid., 3.

38. Ibid., 6.

39. "Clark Rents Cleopatra's Harp for United Artists Film Tour," *Syracuse Post-Standard,* August 14, 1946, LPK-C.

40. Clark, "Harps: My Reason for Collecting Them," January 22, 1949, LPK-C.

41. Clark, autobiographical statement 10, LPK-C.

42. WSYR press release, December 21, 1938, OHA.

43. "Syracusan Finds 'Pigeon Harp,'" *Syracuse American,* October 23, 1938, LPK-C.

44. Clark, "List of Antique Instruments."
45. Ibid.
46. Ibid.
47. Timothy Clark, conversation with author, October 5, 2006.
48. Paul Knoke, conversation with author, October 26, 2006.
49. Clark, "Harps: My Reason for Collecting Them."

Selected Bibliography

IN MAKING THIS BOOK I drew heavily on my own collection of Melville A. Clark papers. I have listed other archival sources below, along with selected books, articles, and newspapers that I consulted.

Archival Sources

Clark, Melville, Papers. Special Collections Research Center, Syracuse University Library, Syracuse, N.Y.

Clark Music Company Records. Special Collections Research Center, Syracuse University Library, Syracuse, N.Y.

Onondaga County Public Library, Syracuse, N.Y.

Onondaga Historical Association, Syracuse, N.Y.

Newspapers

Arizona Republic (Phoenix)

Brooklyn Citizen

Bulletin and Scots Pictorial (Glasgow)

Christian Science Monitor

New York Evening Post

New York Sun

New York Times

Syracuse American

Syracuse Herald

Syracuse Herald-American

Syracuse Herald-Journal

Syracuse Journal

Syracuse Post-Standard

Syracuse Sunday American

Washington Post

Washington Times

Other Sources

Clark, Joan. "Melville Clark and the Clark Irish Harp." *Folk Harp Journal* 96 (1997): 55.

Clark, Melville A. "Music Box for a Princess." *Retail Merchant Magazine,* August 8, 1948.

"Harp under Water." *Life,* December 13, 1948.

Headland, Robert K. *Chronological List of Antarctic Expeditions and Related Historical Events.* Cambridge: Cambridge Univ. Press, 1990.

"How the Syracuse Orchestra Was Born." *Women's Home Companion,* June 1921.

Kramer, Walter A. "Roosevelt and Margaret Wilson in Huge Audience at Syracuse Festival." *Musical America,* May 15, 1915.

Owens, Dewey. *From Aeolian to Thunder.* Chicago: Lyon and Healy Harps, 1992.

"Piano Recording Mechanism." *Musical Age,* February 14, 1911.

"Plastics in Harp Provide Tone Insurance." *Modern Plastics,* November 1951.

Rensch, Roslyn. *Harps and Harpists.* 2nd ed. Bloomington: Indiana Univ. Press, 2007.

Who's Who in America. N.p., 1920.

Index

Italic page numbers denote illustrations. Page locators under Melville Clark's name refer to significant events in his personal life such as marriage, travel, etc.; for other topics relating to Clark's business and professional endeavors (e.g., Syracuse Symphony), please refer to the index entry for that topic.

A. C. Chase Organ and Melodeon Company, 15
Albee, Edward F., 76, 81, 86
amplifier, 69–71, *70, 71*
Apikian, Nevart, 11–12
Apollo Hall, 21, *22*
Apollo player piano, 1, 15
Aptommas, Thomas, 5
assembly plan, children's, 171
Auburn Symphony Orchestra, 11
auto guard, 68–69

balloon offensive project, 99–104, *104*
Bauer, Harold, 79
Becker, Bertha E., *3,* 36
Becker, Conrad, 1
Becker, Conrad L., 1
Becker, Mary, 1
Bernthal, Murray, 94
Berwald, William, 5, 76, 78, 81, *81,* 94
B. F. Keith Theatre, 76, 80, 81, *82,* 87
Bon-Air Silent Motor (BASM), 72
Bond, Augusta, 17

bow, musical, 134, *134*
Brennan, D. T., *77, 78*
Brickman, Jean Marie, *23*
bumper, automobile, 68–69
Byrd, Richard E., 45–47, 49–50

Caesar and Cleopatra, 130
Camp Onondaga, 96–98, *97*
Capehart Automatic Phonograph Company, 67
"Captured Sound" (Clark), 114
Capurso, Alexander, 94
Carothers, Wallace Hume, 55
Carroll, Stephen L., 24
Central New York Music Festival Association, 86, 107
Chapin, Marie Arnold, 89, 94
Chase, Aurin, *77,* 89
Christian Science Monitor, 13, 70, 73, 106, 114
Civic Symphony Orchestra, 91–92
Clark, Arthur, 2–4, *3, 4,* 17–19
Clark, Bertha, 2–3, *3,* 4
Clark, Clarence, 2–3, *3,* 4

Clark, Dorothy E., 8, *10, 11*
Clark, Dorothy Speich, 7–10, *10, 11,* 27, 112
Clark, Ernest, 2–4, *3, 4*
Clark, George W., 1–3, *2, 3,* 14–19, *18,* 29
Clark, Grace, 2–3, *3, 4*
Clark, Lillian Becker, 1, 2, *2, 3*
Clark, Maude, 2–3, *3,* 4, *4,* 109
Clark, Melville, 1, 2, 15, *74a,* 99–100, 101
Clark, Melville A.: bibliography, 141; as cellist, 10–11, *12,* 71; childhood, 1, 2–3, *3, 4, 6;* civic activities, 10, *74b, 74f;* death of, 12–13; Dorothy and, 7–10, *11,* 112; education, 4–6, 29–30; patents (*see* patents); plays at White House, 41, 105–6, 109, 111–12, *112;* religious beliefs, 13; siblings, 2–4; travels abroad, 30, 31–32; war efforts, 96–104; WHEN interview, 123–24; Margaret Wilson and, *107,* 107–9, *109, 110,* 110–11
Clark, Melville, Jr., 8, 9, *10, 11,* 13, 69
Clark, Timothy D., 8, *10, 11,* 27
Clark Baby Grand Harp, 43
Clark Concert Company, 2
Clark Harp Manufacturing Company, 19, 27, 36, 37
Clark Irish Harp: awards, 36; costs, 145–61; description, *33,* 33–34, 51–53; fiberglass, 44, *45,* 59, *74c,* 168n51; genesis of, 31–32, 132; gift to Princess Margaret, 122–23; patents for, 34, *35,* 42–43, 53; played in unusual locations, 44–49, *46, 49, 74c,* 121; promotion, 34–35, *38,* 39–41; reception, 37, 41–42; variations, 42–44

Clark Musical Bureau, 21
Clark Music Company: citation from Admiral Byrd, 49–50, *50;* current status, 27–28; growth, 19–21; harp-related products, 26–27, 30, 34–36, 41; letterhead, *66;* marketing, 23–26; nylon string products, 55–61, *55, 58, 60, 61;* radio ventures, 22–23, *23*
Clark Music Repair Shop, 2, 14
Clark Plan, 23–24
"Cleo" harp, *127,* 130–31, *131*
Clymer, Virgil H., 67
Colville, John, 116–18, *118,* 122, 123
Coman, F. Dana, 45–49, *48, 49*
concert harp. *See* pedal harp
Crabtree, Louis, 87
Crescendo, 41–42
Crouse, Alta Pease, 85
Cudworth, Luther, 12

David, Elizabeth, *109,* 110, *110*
David, Ross, *109,* 110, *110*
Davis, Marion, *109*
De Pavaloff, Henri, 76
Derschung, John, 87, 89
Dilling, Mildred, 135–36
dove harp, 133, *133*
Dudley, Gertrude Woodhall, 90
Du Pont, 55–59, *57,* 61

Eggleston, Spencer, 63
E. I. du Pont de Nemours Company, 55–59, *57,* 61
Elizabeth, Princess, 116–18, 122
Emmet, Robert, 132
Erard harp, 5, *6, 18,* 30, 31
Ethiopian harp, 134–35, *135*

Faunthorpe, J. C., 102–3
fiberglass harp, 42, 44, *45,* 59, *74c,* 168n51
Ford, Henry, 114–15, 129, *130*
Frank, Francis, 93
French harp, 128–29, *130*
Frey, Adolph, 8
From Aeolian to Thunder (Owens), 54
fruit picker, 62–66, *64, 65, 66, 74d*

gang tuning, 42–43
glass harp. *See* fiberglass harp
Grainger, Percy, 79, 90
Groves, Ernie, 9, 69
Gualillo, Nicholas, 93, *93,* 94
G. W. Clark Music Company, 15–18, *16*

Hall O'Harps Monthly, 24, *25,* 41
Harding, Warren G., 79
harmonium, 127
harp collection, Clark's, 128–36
harps. *See specific harp types*
Harps and Harpists (Rensch), 32
Herbert, Victor, 42, 78, 79, 85
Hildebrandt, Eric, 27
Hints for the Guidance of the Amateur Harpist (Morley), 54–55
Honegger, Arthur, 88
Honsinger, Evalina, 87
Hopkins, Carolyn Auth, 95
House, Donald, 125

"Ideas" letterhead, 62, *63,* 72
Instructions for Playing the Harp (Clark Music Company), 35
instrument collection, 125–28

Junge, Henry, 111

Knapp, Martin, 85, 89

lap organ, 126, *127*
lap piano, 125, *126*
Lerner, Tina, 81–84, *83,* 88, *89*
Levee, Myron, 76, *77*
Life, 44, 59, *74c*
Lincoln, Charles M., 99, 100
Logue, Michael Cardinal, 31
Lyman, Howard, 75
Lyon and Healy, 37, 143

MAC Jr., 34
Mackensie, William A., 94
Margaret, Princess, 122–23
Marie Antoinette, 128
marine escape system, 67–68
marking piano, 15
McChesney, Donald S., 89
McCormack, John, 41, 84–85, 105
medieval harp, 30
melodeons, 1–2, 14–15
Miller, Nathan, 79
Miller, Victor, 91, *91*
Montessori, Maria, 41
Morley, J. George, 54–55
Murphy, Hugh Sr., 28
music boxes, *74h,* 114–25, *119,* 121
music education, 21, 23–24
Music Trade Indicator, 78

National Association of Music Merchants, 10, *74b*
National Harp Association, 7

National Harp Festival, 7, *7*
New York Evening Post, 70
New York Times, 59, 60–61
Northcliffe, Alfred Harmsworth,
  Viscount, 102–3
Novachord, 10
nylon harp strings, 43, 54–61, *55, 57,
  58, 60, 61*

Onondaga Council of Girl Scouts,
  21–22
Onondaga Symphony, 95
Osborne, Thomas Mott, 11, 42
Owens, Dewey, 54

Paderewski, Ignaz, 79
Paine, J. Russell, 41
patents: amplifier, 69; auto-related,
  68–69, 72–73; fruit picker, *63,
  64, 65,* 66; gang tuning, 42; Irish
  harp, 34, *35,* 42–43, 53; player
  piano, 15; record changer, 67;
  taborette, 34, 53; trench harp, 43
pedal harp, 26–27, 29, 30–31, 56
phonograph collection, 114, *115*
Piano Trade Magazine, 74b
Pinto, A. Francis, 41–42
Place, William Jr., 7, *7*
Plan of Aerostation, 99–104, *104*
plastic harp. *See* fiberglass harp
Play the Harp (Clark), 36
Polah, André, 91, *92,* 93
Prokofieff, Serge, *74e,* 88
Pulitzer, Ralph, 99, 100

record changer, 67
Rensch, Roslyn, 32

Ripley, Frederick R., 93–94
Ripley's "Believe It or Not," 166n31
Rofgren, C. E., 47, *47*
Rogers, Van Veachton, 4–5, *7,* 35, 37,
  39, *40*
Roosevelt, Franklin D., 111–12
Roosevelt, Theodore, 108

Salzedo, Carlos, 7, *7,* 26, 54
Schirmer, Gustaf, 124
Shavitch, Vladimir, 81–84, *84,* 87, 88,
  89, 90
Singer, Guido, 27
Smith, Maude Mixer, 89
Solovei, Jack, 27
Song and Light Festival, *74f*
stagecoach violin case, 128
stamp collection, *74g,* 113–14
Statue of Liberty, 73
Stokowski, Leopold, 69–70, *70*
Story and Clark, 15
strings, nylon, 43, 54–61, *55, 57, 58,
  60, 61*
Syracuse Federal Symphony, 92–93
Syracuse Journal, 69, 70, 80
Syracuse Philharmonic Society, 94
Syracuse Post-Standard, 11, 59–60,
  94, 128
Syracuse Recruitment Camp, 96–98, *97*
Syracuse String Sinfonietta, 94
Syracuse Sunday American, 86
Syracuse Symphony Orchestra: begin-
  nings, 76–84; decline, 88–91;
  growth, *74e,* 84–88; re-formation,
  94, 95; Syracuse University con-
  nections, 170n2
Syracuse Symphony Orchestra Asso-
  ciation, 93–94
Syracuse University Chorus, 75

taborette, 19, 32, *33,* 34, 52–53
Temple Theatre, 86, 87
Thomas, John, 5, 31
Timothy D. Clark Plastic Harp. *See*
    fiberglass harp
tone amplifier, 69–71, *70, 71*
tortoise shell harp, 135, *136*
Travelers' and Drovers' Tavern, 8–9, *9*
Trench Harp, 43

violin, world's smallest, 127
Visualite, 43, 72
Vito, Elaine, 44, *74c*

Walwrath, John H., 79
Washington Times, 109

Wegeforth, W. Dayton, *77–78*
Welch, Walter L., 114, *115,* 124–25
WHEN, 23
Wilbur, Paul, 67
Wilson, Edith Galt, 109
Wilson, Ellen Axson, 105–6
Wilson, George, *77*
Wilson, Margaret, 41, *98,* 98–99,
    105, *107,* 107–11, *109, 110*
Wilson, Woodrow, 41, 100, 106
Winkler, E. K., 5
Works Project Administration, 92–93
WSYR, 22–23, *23*
Wurlitzer Company, 26

Young People's Concerts, 80, 81,
    86–87, 171